PRAYING TO CHANGE YOUR LIFE

PRAYING TO CHANGE YOUR LIFE

A GUIDE TO PRODUCTIVE PRAYER

SUZETTE T. CALDWELL

DESTINY IMAGE® PUBLISHERS, INC.

P.O. Box 310, Shippensburg, PA 17257-0310

"Speaking to the Purposes of God for this Generation and for the Generations to Come."

This book and all other Destiny Image, Revival Press, Mercy Place, Fresh Bread, Destiny Image Fiction, and Treasure House books are available at Christian bookstores and distributors worldwide.

For a U.S. bookstore nearest you, call 1-800-722-6774.

For more information on foreign distributors, call 717-532-3040.

Reach us on the Internet: www.destinyimage.com.

ISBN 10: 0-7684-2751-7
ISBN 13: 978-0-7684-2751-6

For Worldwide Distribution, Printed in the U.S.A.

4 5 6 7 8 9 10 11 / 13 12 11 10 09

DEDICATION

In memory of my mother, Pastor Gussie L. Turner, who taught me not to put God in a box.

ACKNOWLEDGMENTS

Thank you…

To my Lord and Savior for trusting me to teach and write about His model for prayer.

To my husband, Pastor Kirbyjon Caldwell for believing in and supporting the "call" God has placed on me.

To my children for encouraging me to finish the book.

To Terry Baugh Bessard for working diligently and faithfully with me on this book.

To my "team" for helping me to empower thousands of people to pray through the years.

To my College of Prayer students for learning and applying these prayer principles in their daily lives.

To Pastor Dorothy Brown, Barbara Hicks, and Evangelist Joyce Rodgers for their "attagirls," godly counsel, and unrelenting friendship.

To my Windsor Village UMC Family for their love, support, and prayers.

ENDORSEMENTS

Suzette Caldwell's words come from one whose life has been shaped by prayer. Though written in a common-sense style, she educates us, especially on the use of Scripture in prayer, and provides many helpful examples. Whether you are interested in everyday prayer for yourself or are called on to pray on behalf of a group, Suzette Caldwell's book serves as a great guide, and it also compiles in a readable fashion much of the wisdom Scripture offers on every aspect of our prayer life.

Mayor Bill White
Houston, Texas

My hope is that this book calls a wandering generation back to prayer.

Bishop T.D. Jakes
The Potter's House
Dallas, Texas

All God's people say "Wow!" Suzette's insightful knowledge of prayer will empower you to overcome any obstacles and give you the ability to live the promise-filled life that God has planned for you.

Dr. Robert H. Schuller, Founding Pastor
Crystal Cathedral
Garden Grove, California

For years I have watched in amazement as God has powerfully used the prayer ministry of Mrs. Suzette Caldwell. She and her husband, Pastor Kirbyjon Caldwell, lead a vibrant, loving, Spirit-filled church in Houston, Texas. This is a woman who knows—and has seen—the true power of prayer, and her life and ministry has been revolutionized as a result. I am excited to see how Suzette Caldwell has poured her passion and training into this book, and I know that anyone who reads it will be challenged, encouraged, and blessed while learning how to take their prayer life to a whole new level.

During an evangelistic festival we held in Houston, Suzette led, as you can guess, the great prayer movement surrounding the campaign in that massive metropolis. On site at Eleanor Tinsley Park in downtown Houston, with a crowd of thousands surrounding the prayer tent, scores of pastors came seeking intercessory prayer from this woman and her team. What a glorious sight.

So rejoice in these principles laid out by Suzette Caldwell. Practice them and see God at work through you. "Wait for the Lord; be strong and take heart and wait for the Lord" (Ps. 27:14 NIV).

Dr. Luis Palau, World Evangelist
Luis Palau Association
Portland, Oregon

Pastor Suzette slashes through the moldy red tape that has bound up our churches and hobbled our spirits. In doing so, she unleashes knowledge of the amazing force God gives to everyone who will receive—*prayer!*

Dare to tap into Suzette's prayer help desk! Dare to become God's agent of change! Dare to pray!

Jeff Mosely, CEO/President
Greater Houston Partnership
Houston, Texas

A great book for all Christians! I am excited to learn how to pray productive prayers and learn what God's will is for my life. What a blessing!

Davis Love III
Professional Golfer
St. Simons Island, Georgia

Praying to Change Your Life has deepened my prayer life in three ways: I am practicing using Scripture in prayer much more extensively, I changed the order of my structured devotional time, and I pray with more specificity. Peppered with personal true stories and rich with practical how-to examples, the book is a wonderful guide to the joy that comes from real results from God's Kingdom.

John Montgomery, Founder
Bridgeway Capital Management, Inc.

The Church is in the midst of a massive power failure. Suzette Caldwell believes we've tried to be every kind of Church but the one that counts: a praying Church. Here is a must-read book that moves prayer from a noun to a verb, and a high-octane verb at that, one that overpowers evil while it empowers healing and wholeness.

Dr. Leonard Sweet
Drew University and George Fox University

I have watched with my own eyes the power of prayer in my sister's life. As daughters of a powerful, praying mother, we learned to pray effective prayers practically before we learned to talk. For that, I am most grateful. Effective prayers are specific and deliberate and don't necessarily come naturally to every believer. That is where the value of *Praying to Change Your Life* lies. Suzette has done the work for us in searching out what the Scriptures have to say about who we are in God, how we should communicate with Him, and what we have access to as His children. For the believer who wants to see their prayers touch heaven and activate the Holy Spirit, *Praying to Change Your Life* is a must-read. We all need to understand just how to pray, just as the disciples asked Jesus. This thorough and easily understood primer that *Praying to Change Your Life* provides is not only a spiritual gem but truly an answer to prayers.

Dr. Debbye Turner, DVM
Network News Correspondent
CBS Early Show

Would you like your prayers to be more powerful...and...in line with God's plans and purposes for your life? If your answer is "yes," then you need to read *Praying to Change Your Life: A Guide to Productive Prayer* by Pastor Suzette Caldwell. It's much more than just another book on prayer—it will make your relationship with God more personal and intimate than ever before. In this book, you will discover the important keys that Jesus taught His disciples about prayer and how to apply these principles to your everyday life.

I want to challenge you to read *Praying to Change Your Life*. It will have a long-term impact on your life and position you to be powerfully used by God to accomplish His will on the earth. I believe with my whole heart that if you desire to have a richer, more meaningful prayer life, this book will help you! I highly recommend this book to every believer, regardless of the stage of your prayer life or walk with God.

Dr. Marilyn Hickey
Marilyn Hickey Ministries

Contents

FOREWORD

Welcome to your new world of prayer! For too long, too many people, including believers, have viewed prayer as passive, ambiguous, and intrinsically ineffective. Well, kiss those days good-bye!

As you read *Praying to Change Your Life*, you will experience the Lord's desired intent for prayer: interactive, vibrant, and powerfully effective communication. Pastor Suzette's liberating revelation about The Model Prayer (also known as The Lord's Prayer) can literally transform how you pray, why you pray, and what happens when you pray.

This is not simply another book about prayer. *Praying to Change Your Life* is a God-inspired "go-to guide" for how to see, receive, and perform God's primary will in your personal and professional life.

In The Model Prayer, Jesus says: *"Thy will be done in earth, as it is in heaven"* (Matt. 6:10 KJV). Obviously, there was something going on in Heaven which the Lord wanted re-presented, or represented, on earth. I believe this book has been done in Heaven since the foundation of the world. Now, the Lord is presenting it through Pastor Suzette on earth.

May The Model Prayer be done in *your* life exactly as it is in Heaven!

Pastor Kirbyjon H. Caldwell, Senior Pastor
Windsor Village United Methodist Church

INTRODUCTION

CALLED TO PRAY

Prayer has always been a part of my life. I have taught people how to pray for over ten years, and I have been a student of prayer for more than 15 years.

My mother was a "pray-er." As a child, I watched her literally spend hours on her knees. My sister and I would go to sleep at night, and my mother would just be beginning her prayer time. She would pray into the wee hours of the morning. Sometimes, she would still be praying when we awoke to a new day.

I can still hear her voice as she cried out to the Lord. She would pray for the community or someone who was gravely ill. My fondest memories are of her asking God to bless us, her children; to choose our husbands; to give us the mind and heart of Christ so that we would think and act like Him.

My mother was a model for me in her walk with God. However, in 1991, when the Lord called me to study and teach about prayer, I was intimidated because of what I had seen in my childhood. My mother had dedicated many hours to prayer. I could not imagine spending that many hours on my knees and not running out of things to say to God! I had never been a big talker, so the thought of talking to God at length was incomprehensible. But thankfully, through the years, He has taught me that it doesn't matter *how long* His children pray—although He longs to spend time with them—but that what, in fact, is most important is *what* they say when they pray.

I saw results from my mother's prayers. The truth is, I saw numerous miracles happen. When I was a young girl, a doctor told my mother that I would have to wear orthopedic shoes for the rest of my life due to a genetic defect in the bone structure of my feet. According to him, I would not be able to stand for long periods of time.

One morning around 2 A.M., my mother woke me up and asked me if I believed God could heal my feet. "Yes," I said, "I believe God." She said, "You have witnessed many miracles. Do you believe God can do the same thing for you?" "Oh, yes," I replied.

My mother prayed for me, and the Lord healed my feet that night. When I put my orthopedic shoes on, they no longer fit. The next day we went to the shoe store where special shoes had been ordered for me and the measurements of my feet were kept on file.

As we walked in, the saleswoman who had served me for several years said, "There is something different. I don't know what it is, but there is something different." My mother asked the woman to measure my feet. "They don't fit the measurements," she exclaimed. "My Lord, what happened?" I have not worn orthopedic shoes since that day. God had healed my feet in the wee hours of the morning when Mother prayed. Today, I can wear any type of shoe.

On another occasion, my mother, sister, and I were on our way home from my mother's eye doctor. He had given her a prescription for new glasses because she had been diagnosed with astigmatism. Though she had the prescription filled, she told us that she was not going to wear her new glasses. Instead, she was going to pray and believe God for perfect eyesight.

A few days later, Mother returned to the doctor and asked him to reexamine her eyes. To his amazement, the exam revealed that she had 20/20 vision in both eyes. She left her new glasses with the doctor.

The miracles I witnessed were not limited to my family. When I was about 12 years old, I attended a Full Gospel Businessmen's meeting with my mother at Luby's Cafeteria in Jonesboro, Arkansas. The keynote speaker was a minister who spoke about miracles. He asked for volunteers to help cover his entire face with gauze tape with the exception of one eye. Of the three men who volunteered, one was a doctor. When they finished taping his face, the speaker asked people to bring things for him to read—bills, drivers' licenses, anything.

Several people came forward and the minister proceeded to read from the one eye that was exposed. The miracle of this act was that it was a glass eye, yet he accurately read everything the people brought to him. I was in awe.

Following this exercise, the minister popped out his glass eye and walked around the room showing everyone—including me and a few other children who were in attendance—the pink flesh inside his empty eye socket. He went back to the front of the room and after asking people to again bring him things to read, he started reading from the empty eye socket.

That day I decided I wanted God to use me in an extraordinary way. I too wanted to demonstrate His miracles. Since then, my prayer has always been that God would use me to demonstrate His signs and wonders in order to draw people to Him; God continues to honor this prayer.

Under my mother's tutelage, my sister and I learned to pray using Scriptures. Before praying, Mother would identify the Scriptures we were going to stand on and then intersperse her prayer with the Word as she prayed aloud. She instructed us to believe God's Word and expect results from praying His Word. She told us that God's Word had power and that power produced the results to our prayers. Before she ever prayed, she stated God's Word. Little did I know that her teachings would become the substance of God's calling for my life.

I have been called to pray and to teach prayer in a way that ties people directly to the Word. When you pray, speak what the Scripture is speaking. You don't have to make up words or feel pressured to create something you hope will be pleasing to God. Use His Word, and you will please Him. Use His Word, and you will get powerful results.

CHAPTER 1

PRODUCTIVE PRAYER

I received the diagnosis on January 29, 2004, at approximately 8:30 A.M., that I had breast cancer. The words that came out of the doctor's mouth hit me like a ton of bricks. I could not believe it. I had cancer.

For the next eight hours, I sat in my rocking chair in the bedroom I shared with my husband and cried. It was all I could do. My thoughts were not, "Why me?" or "Woe is me." I never felt that God was punishing me or trying to teach me a lesson. I cried because the news put my emotions into overload, and I was simply overwhelmed.

Around 4 P.M., I remember shaking myself as if to pull myself together. I told myself to stop crying, and I began talking to myself. You have to do that sometimes to make yourself focus so that you can see things more clearly.

You can't always wait to talk issues through with someone else. There are times when you have to reach within yourself and with all the strength you can muster, draw upon your own resolve. Above all else, however, you must reach out to God.

Whose Report Really Counts?

In the midst of my shock and pain, it dawned on me that I had not heard from the Lord. I had been so preoccupied with the diagnosis that I forgot to ask God what His Word was on the matter.

After years of walking with the Lord, I knew how important His Word was to the believer's life. My mother taught me to live on God's Word according to Luke 4:4 which says, *"Man shall not live by bread alone, but by every word of God."*

Hours earlier, I had heard the doctor's report, but I had not received the final report: God's report. It was God's report that would matter most; and it was God's report that would enable me to pray and believe effectively.

So often, believers operate on one report. After receiving an unfavorable report, we must ask God, "What is Your report?" After all, it is the enduring Word that secures our future. It is the Word that causes us to see God's faithfulness clearly. Therefore, it is the Word which will empower us to pray prayers that are *productive* in accomplishing God's will for our lives.

And so I turned from talking to myself to speaking to God. "Father, I heard what the doctor said this morning about this tumor. He said that the biopsy results were positive and the mass is malignant. Lord, what do You say about this?"

Immediately, I heard His voice through the Holy Spirit. His message was clear. First, He said, "You are not going to die." I leaned back into my rocking chair and sighed with relief. This was a wonderful word. I was a young woman with a terrific husband and three beautiful children, and I was not ready to die.

Secondly, He instructed me to walk out the process. I knew, then, that the cancer sitting in my breast was not going to leave my body instantaneously as I would have preferred. This blessed word meant that I would endure the process of undergoing tests, examinations, and surgery. I would have to make repeated visits to the hospital and be counted as one of the sick. For me, someone who never went to the doctor (except to take annual health exams and have children), this word from God would be one of my greatest challenges. That day, I decided in my heart that God would heal me.

There was a third word that the Lord had spoken through the prophet Isaiah thousands of years ago. According to Isaiah 53:5, Jesus was *"wounded for our transgressions, He was bruised for our iniquities; the chastisement for our peace was upon Him, and by His stripes we are healed."* I believed His Word, and I knew that God would heal me.

Revisit Past Victories

The more I tuned into what God was saying, the stronger my faith became and the better positioned I was to pray in productive and power-filled ways.

Hearing God's heart also opened my own heart even more to the history of His faithfulness and, therefore, the promise of His continued faithfulness. Everything that I heard from or about God was preparing me for a new level of effectiveness in prayer. This would prove to be essential in overcoming cancer.

I literally gained strength as I pondered what God said to me that day. Again, I began to talk to myself. I reminded myself of past miracles. I rehearsed in my mind specific miracles that had occurred in my mother's and sister's lives.

God had healed my mother of astigmatism and my sister of an incurable rash. I remembered the miracle that occurred in my mother-in-law's life. For 90 minutes she was pronounced clinically dead. Today, she lives and is vibrant and healthy. I told myself that *"God shows no partiality"*; what He had done for them, I expected He would do for me.

After God spoke His Word to me concerning the cancer, I knew that my total healing and deliverance would come no other way than through prayer. I also knew that it was time to get busy; it was up to me to take hold of what God had showed me, and it was up to me to pray productive prayers that were aligned with what God had already said.

I got up from my chair, went upstairs, and started gathering Scriptures about healing and about what God does for His people when they face crises. I compiled a notebook of Scriptures that I use to this day.

As I gathered the Scriptures, I again heard the Lord's voice. He said, "If the doctor had prescribed medicine, you would have had the prescription filled immediately and would have been taking the medication before the day was over. Take My Word three times a day."

Taking His Word would be my *"balm of Gilead."*² Praying the Scripture would renew my mind, bring my thoughts into agreement with His promises, and increase the favorability of my outcomes.

In other words, God's Word would help me to elevate my *prayer productivity rate*.

God's Multifaceted Provision

It is important to tell you that God did not tell me to refuse any medicine proffered by the doctors. God is the Creator of everything that brings healing—including medicine. I believe that God uses doctors and the medical community to bring about healing. However, God is the only One who can produce the cure.

And so I followed God's prescription—I prayed His Word morning, afternoon, and night. As I underwent natural treatment from the doctors, I took my spiritual medicine.

I confessed the Word over my life, and I trusted God throughout the whole process of preparation for my lumpectomy, which was scheduled for February 10, 2004. There were many check-ups and X-rays and much prodding and poking. When one of the plastic surgeons asked me during a visit if he could open my gown to look at my breast, I told him he might as well, everyone else had.

The health care team at the M.D. Anderson Cancer Center in Houston, Texas, is the best in the world, and the professionals there, who knew much more about breast cancer than I did, wanted to make sure that I knew what to expect.

They explained that they would not know if the cancer had spread until they received the pathology report. If it spread, the cancer was expected to invade my lymph nodes. If this were the case, the lymph nodes would have to be removed, and I would have to worry about my arm swelling.

When I received reports like these, I expressed my appreciation to the messengers, but I told each of them that I expected the opposite outcome. It was not a denial of the knowledge or experience they had, it was a statement of faith.

Face Your Fear

That faith and God's Word carried me through. My mother had taught me to trust God no matter what happened. Philippians 4:6 tells us to *"be anxious for nothing."* That lets us know that there is going to be some anxiety in life.

When a person receives an unfavorable report, it is normal to feel anxious and fearful. These are responses from our flesh. God, who is our Creator, understands this, and He placed provisions within the Scriptures to help us combat these feelings.

Anxiety and fear are enemies of faith. Left unchecked, they will rob you of God's blessings and promises every time. For believers, Second Timothy 1:7 states that *"God has not given us a spirit of fear, but of power and of love and of a sound mind."* In other words, God gave us Himself through the Holy Spirit to overcome the enemies of our healing and deliverance. Through the Holy Spirit, we have power to overcome the bad reports, power to destroy the source(s) of disease, power to call God's plans for healing into the earth, and power to endure the process that we may have to experience in order to reach our deliverance.

When we receive a bad report, we have to pull ourselves together pretty quickly and make a choice. We have to choose life or death. We have to choose whether to trust God and His Word or to put our confidence in the circumstances and ourselves.

I chose life. I chose to trust God and His Word. First, I knew God was going to deliver me because He promises us deliverance. Second, I had seen too many miracles, and I knew He was fully capable of performing one in my life. Third, I rested on the fact that the Lord had called me to do a work and that I had not even touched the tip of the iceberg. He completes what He starts.

In order for God to complete what He had started in me, I had to live. In Psalm 6:4-5, David writes:

Return, O Lord, deliver me! Oh, save me for Your mercies' sake!
For in death there is no remembrance of You; in the grave who
will give You thanks?

I prayed that passage of Scripture to God. I said, "Father, what good am I to You dead? I can do more good for You alive, and You know I am going to lift up Your name and give You the glory for delivering me from this cancer!" I began to expect to live and to praise God for the rest of my life.

The night before surgery, I only had one fear—I was afraid of the anesthesiologist and the power he had to take me from consciousness to unconsciousness and back again. I felt he had too much control over my life. I told God how frightened I was of this fact, and I gave my fear over to Him.

I will never forget what happened. While praying, I saw, in my spirit, a hand waving, and I heard the Lord say, "Be of good cheer. It is I. Don't be afraid." I had preached a sermon on that a couple of weeks prior. After receiving the affirmation from the Holy Spirit, I took my dose of God's Word for the night, went to bed, and slept like a baby.

God's Love Is Unfailing

The next day, I went to the hospital and was prepped for surgery. While I was waiting, the nurse in the holding room wanted to administer a sedative to help me relax. I asked her to wait because I wanted to pray a prayer that I had written the night before. Right before the surgery, the surgical team gathered around me and we prayed. I prayed the way that I have taught thousands of people to pray. On that day, I truly had to walk the talk. After we prayed, the surgical team went to work.

The surgery went well. The oncologist had to take out more tissue than expected. Because of that, the plastic surgeon had to do a lot of maneuvering to preserve my breast.

In recovery, the plastic surgeon came by to make his postoperative checkup. Smiling, he said, "Mrs. Caldwell, you are a praying woman." I told him that I knew the Lord would tell him what to do. He replied, "It's not a matter of what to do. I know what to do. When I walk into the operating room, I just believe God is going to use me to do what needs to be done. And that's what happened with you."

At the time, I was not aware of the plastic surgeon's faith in Jesus Christ. For the remainder of the day, I praised God for placing another faith-filled doctor on my team.

After surgery, there was nothing left to do but wait for the pathology report, which would tell us if all the cancer had been removed. I continued to take the prescription God had given me. Three times a day, I prayed His Word over my life.

Five days later, one of the doctors called. "The Lord really loves you," she said. "Yes, I know that." I responded. "No, you don't understand," she said. "The Lord really loves you and really spoke through you." She said that they could see the miracle that had occurred in my body. She went on to explain that the cancer, one of the most aggressive of its type, sat inside a calcified area that was surrounded by a thinner calcified area. According to this doctor, it was as if those two areas kept the cancer from spreading like it should have.

Because of where the cancer had been positioned—under the fold of the breast and close to the chest wall—if it had spread, it could have entered into a vascular area and eventually into the bloodstream. Praise the Lord—none of this happened. I am thoroughly convinced that God's prescription prevented the cancer from spreading.

I cannot (nor would I try to) explain why some people get their miracle instantaneously and why most people have to go through a process of healing. I do not want to have cancer again, but the experience I went through taught me how to trust God and forced me to use

His Word more than I ever had before. As a result, my prayers were highly productive; the Word of God did not allow the cancer to stay in my body, and I got the opportunity to fully live what I had been teaching others for so long.

Over the years, God has shown me key principles for 21st century praying. You will find them in the chapters that follow. These key principles can transform your prayer life. They will help you to enhance your relationship with God—and when that happens, you can't help but experience an increase in your prayer productivity rate.

Basing prayer on these principles has produced miracles in my life and in the lives of others. I am confident these principles can produce miracles in your life too. I also believe that the uniqueness of what I teach is found largely in the answer to the question I am asked over and over again: *What do you say when you pray?*

By the end of this book, you will understand, not only *why* we are all called to pray, but also *what* we are called to say—and you will have the tools you need to pray effectively, in answer to God's call.

So keep reading! These important subjects *will* be covered. First, let's establish a definition of prayer and explore just what it is that makes prayer so practical and so powerful.

CHAPTER 2

A DEFINITION OF PRAYER

What we are accustomed to calling a prayer
is only a part of it. —Origen

What Is Prayer?

Take a few moments and look back on yesterday. As you reflect on the day and on your actions, can you remember how many times you prayed?

Perhaps you started your morning with a prayer of praise and thanksgiving. Before you stopped for a bite of lunch, you might have closed your eyes and quickly asked for a blessing over your food.

Maybe you were in your car on the way to an important meeting when the traffic congestion prompted you to ask God to clear the way so that you could be on time. Or it could be that, seconds after you got your body in just the right position for a night's sleep, you remembered your promise to pray for your co-worker's ill brother; so you slid out from under the covers and onto your knees.

For some, prayer is a habit introduced to us at an early age by our parents or guardians. We pray because we have been told that it is the right thing to do, and we feel guilty when we don't do it. For others, it is a way to come before the Lord at any time to confess, repent, listen, or ask for something for someone else. Whether you pray less than you think you should or more than most Christians have a desire to, most of us fall short of the Scripture's direction to *"pray continually."*[1]

What does it mean to pray continually? Origen, an early Church father, tells us in words hundreds of years old, that the only practical way to meet the commandment is to combine prayer with duties and duties with prayer.[2]

That might have sounded doable to the people of Origen's day. Life was, no doubt, much slower then. How do we as busy, distracted, technology-driven, global, 21st century followers of Christ, apply Origen's advice today? What exactly is prayer, and why should we make such an ongoing, lifelong commitment to it? What, indeed, is in it for us?

To paraphrase Origen, what most of us call prayer is only a part of it. Often, our thoughts, ideas, beliefs, and even our actions have little to do with what prayer is and much to do with what prayer is not.

For example, prayer is not a posture. "Let us bow our heads," the minister says to prepare us for the prayer to come. We hear the words, "Let us pray," and we all know what to do. We kneel at the altar or at our bedsides or, at times, get on our faces before the Lord. Yet, even when we say "Amen" and come out of our prayer positions, it does not necessarily mean we have prayed.

Neither is prayer an acronym. Many Christians have been taught to pray using the A.C.T.S. "method," which includes Adoration, Confession, Thanksgiving, and Supplication. While these components are key to praying powerful, productive prayers, none taken alone or together is the totality of prayer.

So, then, what is prayer? Simply stated, prayer is a tool that allows us to communicate with God and for God. To gain a fuller understanding of the power and necessity of prayer, though, we must take the definition a little further.

Prayer is a supernatural tool created by God. It allows natural human beings to communicate with Him and for Him so that His plans for our lives (which reside with Him in the supernatural) can be brought to fruition in the natural realm.

In Jeremiah 29:11 God says: "For I know the thoughts that I think toward you, says the Lord, thoughts of peace and not of evil, to give you a future and a hope." In order for us to live out His plans here on earth, they must first be retrieved from the supernatural realm.

He can accomplish His plans and purposes on earth and defeat the plans of the devil through us. To put it in other words, prayer is the supernatural vehicle that transports us back and forth between the natural and supernatural realms in order to extract God's plans for our lives and make them into earthly realities.

Supernatural vehicle? Communicate for Him? Accomplish His plans and purposes (and not ours)? Defeat the plans of the devil? Those are not words normally used to describe what is commonly called prayer. Yet, those very words and their meanings will help us to more clearly see prayer for what it really is—the center of Christian living.

Going Where No One Has Gone

"Could there be life out there?" Finding the answer to that question has been the driving force behind man's ongoing and relentless exploration of outer space. The NASA space program was created to discover the possibilities that outer space offers.

However, in order to carry out its mission, NASA had to produce a variety of vehicles that would transport human beings from their natural environment (earth) to a foreign environment (outer space).

One of these vehicles is the space shuttle. It carries human beings known as astronauts into outer space to explore and "capture" the possibilities and bring them back for earthly consideration. This is one of the ways in which NASA accomplishes its mission.

From His control base in the supernatural realm, God achieves His mission through the plans He has set for each of our lives. As stated earlier, God's plans for our lives are with Him in the supernatural. In order to experience His plans, we must work with Him to make them earthly realities. We do this through prayer.

Prayer is our space shuttle; it is the vehicle we must use to gain access to God's environment. When we open our mouths to pray, we launch the vehicle of prayer into His realm. Once there, we are able to retrieve the plans and purposes He wants accomplished for us and bring them to the earth.

To successfully complete God's mission, our prayer vehicles must be loaded with a special rocket payload—a power source that can get this supernatural job done. That payload is the Word of God. And just as every component of space travel (including fuel, hardware, software, and skilled astronauts) has a specific job description to accomplish NASA's overall mission, God's Word "works" to accomplish the mission at hand in our lives.

God's Word has multiple functions comprising its job description. Once we load His Word into our prayers, those functions are set in motion. Chapter 4, "The Power Source," discusses the Word's job description in detail.

Please note that, as you read this book, it is important for you to put on your "faith cap." Through faith you will better understand this concept of prayer and how God uses it to achieve His purposes. We may not always understand how God's mechanisms work, but we know by faith that they do work. While we cannot see or touch prayer, we know it operates and produces results.

Why Should We Pray?

We pray to communicate with God. Prayer gives us direct access to the Lord. During the time of the Old Testament, the masses did not have this privilege because the way to God had not yet been fully opened. Although an Israelite was one of God's chosen people, he still had to rely on a specially appointed representative of God to hear from God and to communicate back with Him through sacrifices and offerings.

But as Jesus declared about Himself: *"I am the way, the truth and the life. No one comes to the Father except through Me."*[3] Jesus' death on the cross opened up the way to the Father. Everyone who believes in His Son can, in turn, reach out to God through prayer.

Yet in our reaching out, most of us have been taught to do so only for what we wish to achieve. It is true that God wants a close relationship with us and that He hears us when we cry out to Him and share with Him our most intimate longings and desires.

God-focused prayer, however, is not about asking the Lord for the things that we want. It is actually about asking Him what He wants done through us. That is why He created prayer. God created it as the vehicle for accomplishing His will on the earth. Through prayer, God partners with the believer to manifest His purposes. We consult with Him about His plan of action for the day. Through this partnership, our relationship grows and becomes more intimate. It is in our best interest to learn as much as we can about the nature and the power of this vehicle so that His will is done.

Prayer is a supernatural vehicle. For some people, the word *supernatural* may seem spooky, conjuring up feelings of fear, mysticism, or evil. But it cannot be any of those things because it belongs to God who is supernatural. The prefix *super* means "over" or "above."[4] Therefore, the word *supernatural* means "above the natural." God lives in a realm above the natural realm in which you and I currently live. Our realm consists of physical matter—flesh, sun, sky, earth, organic and inorganic material. Everything that can be experienced through our five senses is part of the natural realm.

By becoming flesh in the person of Jesus Christ, God bridged the natural and supernatural realms for us. Jesus knew what it was to be like us, spirits housed within physical bodies. He returned to His Father as a spirit, and He dwells in the supernatural realm. Though we live in the natural realm, through Jesus Christ, our spirits can connect with the Spirit of God in the supernatural realm. Jesus said:

> But the hour is coming, and now is, when the true worshipers will worship the Father in spirit and truth; for the Father is seeking such to worship Him. God is Spirit, and those who worship Him must worship in spirit and truth.[5]

How do we worship God in spirit and in truth? We do it by laying down our Christian traditions in order to see things the way our supernatural God sees them. And we do it by answering His call for a pure understanding of prayer—an understanding that can only be achieved through the study of His Word and a longing to connect with His Spirit.

We pray to partner with God. Why would God grant us the awesome privilege of being in partnership with Him? He allows us this relationship so that His plans might come to pass on earth. (Don't tell anyone, but the following information is classified. Put in the right hands, this information could revolutionize the world. It could literally change life as we know it. Please handle this information carefully!)

Contrary to what many people may believe, prayer was created for God's purposes. Prayer was not created to chase the world's problems, your problems, or my problems. It was designed to manufacture, or manifest, God's promises for the world. It is the vehicle that He uses to accomplish His plans for our lives.

Throughout the centuries, prayer has been relegated to a self-serving practice with *"me"* as its central focus. Quite frankly, a one-sided conversation about one person becomes old and trite over time. Although prayer has been used as the platform for expressing self-pity, doubt and unbelief, dissatisfaction, cowardice, and selfishness, God always intended prayer to be the conduit for His will.

In Matthew 26:36-46, we see Jesus agonizing over the events that are about to occur in His life. After three years of teaching, preaching, and performing miracles, His greatest challenge was still ahead.

Jesus was aware of the final directives of His calling on earth, so He found a quiet place to pray in the Garden of Gethsemane. With much distress, He expressed His innermost feelings to God, His Father, and wished that the cup that was before Him would pass. With sweat pouring from His brow as thick as blood droplets, He said, *"Not as I will but as You will."*

Through these words, Jesus connected and partnered with God in accomplishing the final act for humankind. Jesus' prayer was not self-centered, although His suffering would have warranted self-focus. Instead, His prayer was God-centered.

When we pray, our prayers are to be God-centered too. Our focus should be on God's business. What does God want to accomplish for the day? What needs to be said in our prayers that will cause His plans in the supernatural to become our reality?

Please do not misunderstand this point. God is extremely interested in hearing about the happenings of our lives. He wants us to come to Him when we are in need. He wants to hear our desires, but He also wants us to hear His desires, and He wants us to work with Him to achieve His desires. When His desires are fulfilled, our desires are satisfied.

Matthew 6:33 gives us a clue about attending to God's business, first: *"But seek first the kingdom of God and His righteousness, and all these things shall be added to you."* When our prayer lives are centered on what God wants, our conversations with Him and for Him will become more interesting. Prayer becomes more of a joy than an obligation. Additionally, our needs are met as we seek His business first. It is through our partnership with God that our relationship grows and becomes more intimate. Like a master carpenter working with an apprentice, God shares His wisdom, knowledge, and experience to help us become more skillful at doing His work. The master/apprentice relationship requires time spent together; the sharing of valuable principles, methods, and techniques; and actions based upon what has been learned. This type of day-to-day relationship produces trust, confidence, and companionship. As you work with God to pray His interests, you will experience His loving-kindness and tender mercies. Your relationship will flourish into a warm, loving friendship.

Stop for a moment and think about your prayer conversations with God. In your talk with Him, who is your primary focus? Is your conversation filled with words that express what God wants or what you desire? How much of your prayer time is spent telling Him about your shortcomings and insecurities and asking Him to do something for you?

Over the years, as my team of instructors and I have put into practice the idea of first attending to God's business, we have noticed that our lists of "wants" has decreased, our time with the Lord has become more enjoyable, and our prayers are more productive. Jeremiah 29:11-12 states:

For I know the thoughts that I think toward you, says the Lord, thoughts of peace and not of evil, to give you a future and a hope. Then you will call upon Me and go and pray to Me, and I will listen to you.

The plans of God for our lives are with Him in the supernatural realm. In order for us to retrieve His plans from the supernatural, we must use the supernatural vehicle called prayer. Prayer takes us into the supernatural and returns His plans back to the earth.

It is important to note that prayer is a vehicle designed to transport words about God and His Kingdom. When it is filled with any other type of "cargo," such as expressions that are not aligned with God's Word, the vehicle quickly becomes compromised and "out of compliance."

This alignment with God's Word is critical to a productive prayer life. When we partner with God, we link our arms in His arms and agree with Him in whatever He says, believes, thinks, and desires. We must go where He goes and do what He commands us to do. We will know how to be His ideal partners through productive prayer that is based in His Word.

The importance of the Word cannot be underestimated. Problems arise anytime our communication with God is focused on our presumptions. When pray-ers focus on their own ideas, they eventually discover that God is going in one direction and they are going in another.

Too often, we want the Lord to agree and act on our traditions, opinions, and misquotes of His Word. We expect God to partner with us, instead of the other way around. That kind of misguided expectation creates tension in our relationship with God.

I remember playing tug-of-war when I was a little girl. I loved the challenge of overcoming the strength of the opposing team. I tried my best to choose for my team those friends who appeared to be bigger and stronger. Before starting the game, we would dig our heels in the ground and try to position our bodies so that we could make the "maximum pull." With our teeth clenched and fingers wound around the rope so tightly that our knuckles turned white, someone would holler, "Go!" and we would pull as hard as we could.

My team would pull one way, and the opposing team would pull the other. For a few minutes, we would sway back and forth until the force of our pulling stretched the rope taut. At that point, it would appear that no one was winning; both teams were pulling with equal strength. With sweat pouring from our brows, we pulled, but didn't go anywhere. The tension in the rope was so tight that you could bounce a quarter off of it. This is the kind of tension that is produced in our lives when we attempt to pull God in our direction.

Now, take a moment and think about your life. Is it always filled with stress and tension? Do you find yourself trying to convince God to follow you when all the while He is wooing you to follow Him? Are you acting out your life based on God's Word and instructions, or have you convinced yourself that your way is God's way? Do you live under the cliché that says, "If it's not one thing, it's another"?

If you answered "Yes" to any of these questions, then, I want to suggest that you check the condition of your partnership with God. A strained walk with God does not bring abundance.

When we experience perpetual stress in our lives, it would do us good to check in with God to see whether we are fully in partnership with Him. When we are aligned with God, He can provide strength and bring harmony to any crisis. Ecclesiastes 4:12 describes the staying power of this kind of partnership saying, *"A threefold cord is not quickly broken."*

A partnership with God means that we yield to Him. "Whatever You say, Lord," should be our immediate reply to His requests and to His Word. Consider the following responses to God's leading:

"Lord, no one has taught me how to heal, but if the Bible says that I have the power to lay hands on the sick and expect them to recover, then it will be done."

"Your Word says to pray for my enemies who despitefully use me. That's a tough assignment, but I am in agreement with You and I will do my best."

"You want me to work in the prison ministry for a season and be diligent about it so that You can accomplish Your will in the lives of the people we will touch? My answer is, 'Yes and amen!'"

When you enter into your prayer time, approach God from this perspective: "What do I need to say so that God's plans for today will be implemented?" With God, even the seemingly impossible will become possible. Through Christ, who gives us strength, we can stand as full partners and do all things that God commands us to do.

A Praying Partnership

"Bring all the tithes into the storehouse, that there may be food in My house, and try Me now in this," says the Lord of hosts, "[and see] if I will not open for you the windows of heaven and pour out for you such blessing that there will not be room enough to receive it."[6]

As partners with the Lord, we don't get to pick and choose which commands or directives we will agree to obey. For instance, believers are commanded to pay a 10 percent tithe on earnings. For some of us, this is a difficult instruction to follow. I have heard people say that it is all right to start at 2 percent and work up to 10 percent. However, giving less than 10 percent violates our partnership with God.

On the other hand, giving 10 percent demonstrates our faith in that partnership. As a result, there will not be enough room to receive God's blessings, and the devourer (the devil) will be rebuked for our sake.

I have a personal story to share about the benefits of tithing. While shopping at a department store one day, I took my wedding rings off and put them in my purse. Before leaving the store's parking garage, I looked in my purse to get the rings and could only find one of them. I took everything out of my purse and checked the lining for holes; there were no holes. The other ring was gone. I retraced my steps where I had shopped and even enlisted the garage attendant to help me search. However, our efforts were in vain. When I got home, I went through my purse again and found nothing.

That night I prayed, "God, I really love those rings, and You know how much they mean to me. I need Your help. Please do not let Kir-byjon (my husband) notice that I have lost one of my rings." (Isn't it amazing what we will pray?) The next day, I called the department store to see if anyone had turned in my ring. Unfortunately, no one had.

As I sat and thought about my predicament, I remembered a story told by Mrs. Sheila Arthurs, who co-pastors Wheaton Christian Center with her husband, Pastor Carlton Arthurs.

While they were on a trip, they stopped at a gas station to refuel their car and buy snacks. It wasn't until they reached their home in Chicago that they discovered Pastor Arthurs' wallet was missing.

Mrs. Arthurs told her husband not to worry because he was a tither and tithers have the devil rebuked for their sake. She went on to say that the devourer could not harm them and that their storehouse was always full. She was confident that the wallet would be found, and she told Pastor Arthurs so. The story ends with the wallet being mailed to Pastor Arthurs with everything still in it.

Encouraged by the Arthurs' testimony, I offered up another prayer to the Lord and said, "Lord, I am a tither, and You said that if we tithe, the devourer would be rebuked for our sakes. I believe Your Word. I believe that my ring will be found."

About five days later, I was looking for something in my purse, not even thinking about my wedding ring. There, at the bottom of the purse, was the missing ring. I cannot explain it other than to say that when our actions are in agreement with God's Word, our partnership with Him pays off!

We pray to release God's Word into the earth. The Body of Christ is the mouthpiece for God. As believers, we are the "voice" that God uses to speak on earth. When we speak His Word, He is able to speak in the earth. When we do not verbally utter His promises, commands, and instructions, God is unable to articulate them on earth.

God's Word must be heard in Heaven and on earth. God used Moses and Aaron to tell Pharaoh to set His people free from Egyptian bondage.[7] God directed Ezekiel to speak to dry bones so that the people of Israel would, once again, become a thriving community.[8] God spoke through the man, Jesus Christ, to bring Good News to a dying world.[9]

The use of our voices is one of the ways that God partners with us to accomplish His will. As the Sovereign, Almighty God, He does not "need" human beings, but He has chosen to partner with us to fulfill His purposes.

What a marvelous thing to think about the fact that God wants to partner and work with us! It is beyond comprehension. But praise God; what an awesome testament it is of His love for us!

Spoken, Word-filled prayer has power and causes God's will to be done on the earth. It is the engine that advances the Kingdom of God on earth. The Bible says that He watches over His Word and that it moves swiftly to do His work. He is bound to answer His own Word.

Whatever situation you are going through, pray out loud with the force of His Word, and your prayer will produce God's plans for your life in His way, in His time. Lend God your voice and watch His plans multiply in your life.

God's plans for our lives and for humankind are with Him in the supernatural. To hear and receive those plans, as well as His promises and blessings, we are required to enter into His realm. In His infinite wisdom, God has created the perfect means of transportation to do just that: prayer.

How Should We Pray?

What do we say when we pray? The thought of going before the Almighty Lord can be intimidating in itself, but when we have to make sure to say the right words in the right way, it can be enough to stop (or at least slow down) any good Christian from praying. We may end up feeling it would be easier to just dabble in prayer and leave the real praying to those we see as having been "anointed and appointed" to pray. In reality, all believers must pray, and every believer can pray in a way that blesses God and produces His results.

There are some people who feel they don't have to pray much because they receive blessings anyway. They don't know that their blessings came because God had somebody else pray for them—somebody who understood what needed to be spoken in order to accomplish

God's will for their life. He loves us enough to maintain and sustain us until we learn how to communicate effectively through prayer.

Jesus takes prayer very seriously. His actions at the Temple demonstrate His reverence for prayer:

> *Jesus went into the temple of God and drove out all those who bought and sold in the temple, and overturned the tables of the money changers and the seats of those who sold doves. And He said to them, "It is written, 'My house shall be called a house of prayer,' but you have made it a 'den of thieves.'"*[10]

Jesus was angry about the activities transpiring in the Temple and He made His anger known.

This reminds me of a time when I was a young girl. I had gotten into trouble for something that I cannot remember and my mother gave me a spanking for it. I call it the "walk and talk spanking."

As she was spanking me, we were moving in one direction together and she was talking, all at the same time. As she was speaking, her words followed the rhythm of her swings, creating a syncopated motion as she declared: "Suzette…I…asked…you…not…to…do…this… and…I…expect…you…to…do…better."

In my mind, I can see Jesus, as He whipped the money changers out of the Temple, saying, "It…is…written…my…house…shall… be…called…a…house…of…prayer,…but…you…have…made…it… a…den…of…thieves." I believe Jesus got His point across to them that day.

In that day, when Jesus spoke those stinging words, He was referring to a physical structure—the Temple from which He had just driven the merchants and the money changers. But He was also speaking prophetically about the structure to come—the human temple. The

Bible states in First Corinthians 3:16 that *"you are the temple of God and...the Spirit of God dwells in you...."*

We are houses of prayer. When Jesus completed His mission on earth, the material structure of the Temple changed from brick and mortar to flesh and blood. Every believer is a command center that is to receive and transmit godly communications. All believers have a part to play in communicating God's will *"on earth as it is in heaven."* Each believer must pull his or her load in prayer. The sum of all the parts produces the whole of God's will for humanity.

It is worth noting that Jesus did not say that His house was to be a house of *preaching*, a house of *praise and worship*, or a house of *programming*. Preaching, praising, and programming are vital to the life of the Church, but prayer must be at the center of all we do.

Having prayer at the center of our lives provides the foundation to answer the question: *How should we pray?* The answer is simple: let us pray—not halfheartedly, not repetitively, not timidly—but as true disciples steeped in faith, armed with the Word, led by the Holy Spirit, and strengthened by who we are in Christ.

To pray prayers that get results, you don't have to be gifted, but just committed to continuous improvement in your prayer life.

Effective, Fervent Prayers

The effective, fervent prayer of a righteous man avails much. [11]

Powerful, productive prayer is effective (or *effectual*) and fervent. The Greek word for the phrase "effectual, fervent" is *energeo*, which essentially means to be operative, to be at work, or to put forth power. [12] Webster's definition for the word *effective* is to "produce the intended or expected result." [13]

When we pray, our prayers need to hit the nail square on the head and produce God's intended results. When God's Word is loaded into prayer, we are effective. When we pray God's Word, we are certain to be accurate and productive every time. God's Word knows where to go in the supernatural and how to reach His plans. We simply have to speak it out.

The word *fervent*, as defined by Webster, is "having or showing great warmth or intensity of spirit, feeling, enthusiasm, etc."[14] Fervent prayers are passionate, hot, fiery, and eager. We don't have to check our emotions in at the door when we enter the throne room to pray. God welcomes our fervent prayers. He is closer than the breath we breathe. He already knows what we are feeling, whether it is happiness, sadness, excitement, anger, or fear. We are able to feel those emotions and many more because He designed them.

To go before Him masking what is truly in our hearts and on our minds is to treat Him as far less than the friend He wants to be to us. This kind of denial of our emotions also renders us powerless to make a change.

Too often, we show more emotion at the baseball park, football stadium, nightclub, rock concert, gambling casino, or horse races. We get excited when we hear good news, win a prize, get a promotion, or accomplish a goal. Yet, when it comes to God, we believers are too often quiet, sullen, solemn, and even sterile in our approach to Him.

If our best friends talked to us the way we talk to God, how long would we have them as best friends? Don't we talk to the people we love, the ones who we confide in, with expression, emotion, and passion? That is how God wants us to talk to Him. He wants our prayers to be energetic, expressive, and exciting. If you are excited about something when you pray, let Him hear and see your excitement. If you are happy, be happy with God, and let your voice and body language exude your happiness. If you are feeling sadness, express your feelings and allow Him to share your sentiment. Sadness is probably the single emotion that God hears from believers regularly. It is alright to share our sadness, but God wants the full gamut of our emotions to be verbalized in our prayers.

Be real with the Lord. Put everything on the table, but don't forget who you are talking to. He is the Most High God, willing and able to answer your prayer. Nothing is impossible for Him, but we must do our part.

So Jesus answered and said to them, "Assuredly, I say to you, if you have faith and do not doubt,…if you say to this mountain, 'Be removed and be cast into the sea,' it will be done. And whatever things you ask in prayer, believing, you will receive."[15]

We can believe we will receive what we pray for when we pray God's Word. His Word brings results. Idle words have no power. God never told us to climb up the mountain. He never said to burrow through the mountain, go around the mountain, or even dig under the mountain.

He said to *speak* to the mountain and it would move!

CHAPTER 3

TO WHOM DO WE PRAY?

Where can I go from Your Spirit? Or where can I
flee from Your presence? If I ascend into heaven,
You are there; if I make my bed in hell, behold
You are there. —Psalm 139:7-8

To ask "To whom do we pray?" does not pose a trick question or initiate an empty exercise. The answer to the question is at the foundation of our prayers.

We pray to the Lord, but do we really know who He is? Who is this God who created the heavens and the earth and all that exists in between and whose very Word does not rest until it obeys Him?

A review of His characteristics, as revealed through Scripture, gives us a sense of the kind of God we serve. Consider the following seven characteristics of the author, God.

God Is Eternal

*But You, O Lord, shall endure forever, and the
remembrance of Your name to all generations.*[1]

God has always existed. There is no beginning to God, and there
will be no end. He "shall endure forever"!

It can be a mind-blowing exercise to attempt to grasp the concept
of eternity with our finite intellects. Think about it. God, who created
the beginning, has no beginning and does not end. He has always
existed, ungoverned and unlimited by time. He wasn't created, so He
cannot be destroyed. He cannot deteriorate, but we can, because we are
bound by time. We exist in a swatch that God took out of eternity. He
put us in it and created time. Ever since then, life and death have been
a part of our human existence at His will.

*Before the mountains were brought forth, or ever You had formed
the earth and the world, even from everlasting to everlasting, You
are God.*[2]

We can't help but marvel at a God who is timeless but uses time for
His purpose and to His glory. Thousands of years ago, Abraham was
promised by God that his descendants would someday be as great as the
sands of the sea. In the 21st century, His promise continues to live.

God Is Omnipotent

*God has spoken once, twice I have heard this: that
power belongs to God.*[3]

God is power, and He possesses all power. All power comes from
God: nuclear power, hydropower, military power, governmental power.
Ultimately, He created all power, and He can use it for His purposes.
All power in Heaven and on earth is His.

Ah, Lord God! Behold, You have made the heavens and the earth by Your great power and outstretched arm. There is nothing too hard for You.[4]

The light company bills us and collects our payments, but electricity is powered by God. Our votes put elected officials in office, but governmental power comes from the Lord. The power of God has no limits or constraints. His power can heal the deadliest disease and raise the dead. Psalm 93:4 states that the Lord *"is mightier than the noise of many waters, than the mighty waves of the sea."* Military might does not hold a candle to God's omnipotence. See the nations in the world; the power of God surpasses them all.

There is nothing too difficult for God. He is able to overcome any obstacle and destroy any hindrance. The power of disease, sickness, famine, poverty, oppression, arrogance, abuse, pride, and greed cannot exceed His power; it is His power that will eradicate the powers that come to destroy His people.

Power—God provides it, and we harness it.

God Is Omnipresent

> *Where can I go from Your Spirit?*
> *Or where can I flee from Your presence?*
> *If I ascend into heaven, You are there;*
> *If I make my bed in hell, behold, You are there;*
> *If I take the wings of the morning,*
> *And dwell in the uttermost parts of the sea,*
> *Even there Your hand shall lead me,*
> *And Your right hand shall hold me.*[5]

God's omnipresence can be another difficult concept to grasp. God is present, everywhere, at every time in history.

God is everywhere! He is in the heavens—even the farthest reaches of outer space—and in the deepest parts of the ocean. It amazes me to think that there is an entire kingdom in the deepest depths of the oceans, which humans know nothing about. And yet, God is there. God rules in the deepest, blackest parts of the ocean; He is present there, even among life forms that humans have never seen. God's greatness and sovereignty extend far beyond what we could even imagine.

So many times, we human beings relegate God to our own humanness. We often tend to think that God can do about as much as—or perhaps a little more than—we can do.

When we build a skyscraper, we may view it from the ground up and think, *"Look how tall it is!"* We think that must be how big God is. Since we have begun to send men and women into space and explore that territory, we tend to think that God must exist at least that far out into the universe. When we drill down deep into the earth, we suddenly realize that God is there also. No matter where humans will one day travel, no matter how far into the universe they will explore, God will always exist farther than that!

God is so much greater than any achievement of humankind. He is beyond our intellect. As big as we can conceive Him to be, He is bigger than that! And we must treat Him as such. God isn't bound by our earthly problems. He certainly cares about what each one of us is going through, and His heart breaks when we are hurting or in trouble, but He is not constrained by the problems of this life. When we relegate God to what we can do in our own humanity, we miss out on the greatness of God in our lives.

In addition to being present in the outskirts of the universe and in the lowest reaches of the sea, God is also present where you are. For most of us, that is a comfort—He is with us when we need Him the most. But God doesn't just show up when we ask Him to—He is ever-present in every place.

God Is Omniscient

Great is our Lord, and mighty in power; His understanding is infinite.[6]

God's omniscience makes Him all-knowing. Nothing is beyond His understanding; no situation, process, or event is unknown to Him. He will never be surprised by anything because He knows everything—past, present, and future!

As time goes on, the Lord reveals more and more of the things of life, yet men continue to say, "We discovered this," or, "We invented that." In reality, God knew it was there all along—because He put it there! God knows everything.

Not only does God know everything there is to know about our world and the universe in which we live, but He also knows everything about each of us. He even knows the number of hairs on our heads! He knows what makes us happy, and He knows what disappoints us. He understands the deepest yearnings of our hearts and hears our quiet thoughts.

As parents, when we see our children struggling over things that we have experience and knowledge about, we wonder why they won't ask for our guidance and instruction.

We could make their lives so much easier. We could help clear their way of obstacles that hinder them from being all that they are called to be.

Put God in your place. He wants the same things for each of us. And let's face it: His knowledge is beyond compare; what we think we know is nothing compared to what He knows.

God's infinite knowledge is available to us—we just need to ask Him for His help. If you are frustrated in your job, go to the Lord and ask Him what to do. Consult with Him about your projects. He can increase your knowledge and give you new and better ideas on how to get things done.

If you are in school, pray and ask God to give you His understanding of the classes you are taking. God is the designer, the Creator of everything you are studying. He holds all of the knowledge in the universe, and He is willing to impart wisdom and understanding to His children when they ask Him for it.

God Is Righteous

The Lord is righteous in all His ways, gracious in all His works.[7]

God is without sin and does not commit errors of any kind. When He makes a decision, it is always right. His grace and His mercy, as well as His judgments, are always right.

When people read the Old and New Testaments, many of them become confused at what seems to be a stark difference between the two. The Old Testament can seem to be quite bloody—even gory at times! Clearly, in the Old Testament, justice reigned. Christ had not yet come, and God's justice and punishment for sin were much more marked and obvious.

Interestingly, however, there is no contradiction between the Old and New Testaments. God's grace was still present in the Old Testament—especially when we read of the promises of a coming Savior. His justice is still present in the New Testament, because without acceptance of Christ's sacrifice, we are doomed.

In each case, whether justice or mercy seems to prevail, God continues to be right. He is right in both His judgment of our sins and in

His offer of the grace that has been purchased through the blood of His Son, Jesus.

God Is Truth

He is the Rock, His work is perfect; for all His ways
are justice, a God of truth and without injustice,
righteous and upright is He.[8]

God is Truth. That means He is fundamentally incapable of lying. He will never do anything that is contrary to His Word, for that would cause Him to be a liar, something He can never become.

Everything God has said is true and is Truth. For that reason, if you are studying something that does not line up with the Word of God, it is not Truth; it is the knowledge of man.

The knowledge of man often contradicts the truths found in the Word of God, but ultimately it will never hold a candle to what the Lord has said. Many of the great philosophers that we have studied in school—Socrates, Plato, Aristotle, St. Aquinas, Descartes, Nietzsche— as well as all of the mythology and religions of the world, have provided knowledge. Yet, if their knowledge does not align with Scripture, then it is not Truth.

Even some modern-day "philosophizers," who have authority and influence in today's society, fail, at times, to follow what the Scriptures teach. Their teachings and philosophies may sound good, and they may even make a bit of sense, but if they do not line up with the Word, they are not Truth.

It is so important for the Church today to understand this funda- mental reality: God will always agree with His Word. The knowledge of man is all around us in our society—through television programs, movies, music, billboards, advertisements, the news media, and the list goes on. We must constantly judge what we see and hear by holding it up against the measuring rod of the Scriptures.

While we are not called to conform to the world, we are called to live in it. It's important to have some understanding of the culture and the society in which we live; otherwise, how would we ever be able to relate to or reach an unbeliever where they are?

It is also important to understand what the people around us are thinking—and so it is wise to read books on philosophy, or take a class on world religions, or watch the news at the end of the day, as long as you are doing so with a strong foundation already set in God's Word.

Christians need to remain rock solid in their faith and in the Truth that is the Word of God, but they also must be able to reach out from that place of Truth and influence the world around them.

God Is Faithful

Jesus Christ is the same yesterday, today and forever.[9]

God never changes! And He *"shows no partiality."*[10] What He did for those who were faithful to Him in the Bible, He wants to do for us today!

Sometimes that truth is hard for many of us to grasp. We are born into human families that make mistakes and to parents who often treat children with favoritism. It's hard not to. It is human nature to gravitate toward those with whom we enjoy spending time or toward those whom we believe are most like us.

But God doesn't gravitate to one of His children more than to the others! He loves each of us equally and infinitely. God may give more responsibility to those who have shown that they can be trusted, but that certainly doesn't mean that He loves them any more than He loves the rest of us. As a matter of fact, He will tend to help out the person who is lacking in order to bring them up to a level of trustworthiness and responsibility!

God is faithful. All of the promises that God has made to us in His Word can be relied upon. All of the promises that God has made to His faithful children in the Scriptures also apply to us today. God promised Abraham, thousands of years ago, that his descendants would someday be as great as the sands of the sea.[11] Today, in the 21st century, His promises to Abraham are still in force. We can count on His promises, because He is faithful.

The most amazing thing about this list of God's characteristics, when we are considering the subject of prayer and the Word, is that all seven of these attributes of God also apply to His Word!

God's Word is eternal, omnipotent, omnipresent, omniscient, righteous, truthful in every way, and faithful. When God's Word is incorporated into our prayers, His attributes—the characteristics that convey who He is—begin to work in the supernatural and manifest the products of our prayers.

CHAPTER 4

THE POWER SOURCE

The grass withers, the flowers fade,
but the Word of our God stands forever.
—Isaiah 40:8

My dad came to visit one weekend to see our children play in their basketball and baseball leagues. Instead of Dad having to rent a car, I offered him our family's old Toyota Sequoia. We had purchased a new car, and the Sequoia was just taking up space in the driveway.

A few days before my dad's arrival, my husband decided to fill the tank with gas, take it to the car wash, and get the oil checked. When he turned the ignition the car would not start. He tried it again, but there was no sound. The battery was dead. After sitting for months, it had lost its charge. Blessedly, a family friend was at the house and she gave the car a jumpstart. In just a few minutes, my husband was on his way.

Like our cars, prayer requires a power source to operate. The power source, or battery, for our prayers is God's Word. Prayer that is loaded with God's Word is charged with life and power. That life and power causes prayer to enter into the supernatural realm, retrieve God's plans for our lives, and bring them back into the natural realm to be manifested as earthly realities.

God's people are required to pray efficacious, powerful prayers. So many Christians have a lackluster, ineffective prayer life because they do not incorporate the Scriptures into their prayers. When you use the Word of God in your prayers, you will experience positive results.

The Author of the Word

According to Paul's letter to Timothy, The Word of God was created by God:

All Scripture is given by inspiration of God, and is profitable for doctrine, for reproof, for correction, for instruction in righteousness, that the man of God may be complete, thoroughly equipped for every good work.[1]

The entire Bible was created by God. There are those people who would like to discredit Scripture by professing it to be full of errors and declaring that it contradicts itself. But the Word of God was never meant to be completely understood by the human mind alone: God gave us the Holy Spirit to help reveal the Bible's meaning and apply it to our lives. It is trustworthy and reliable for us in every area of our lives today.[2]

God is the author of Scripture. The Greek word for "inspiration" found in Second Timothy 3:16 is *theópneustos*, which means "God-breathed."[3] Every time God breathes into or onto something, He infuses it with life.

Scripture tells us that, after He created Adam, God breathed life into his being:

And the Lord God formed man of the dust of the ground, and breathed into his nostrils the breath of life; and man became a living being.[4]

As God-breathed creations, we carry His image upon us. Because He is the author of His Word, it also bears His image. When we carry God's Word into our prayers, we become partners with Him, equipped for every good work and able to breathe life into our world.

The Word Became Flesh

Much of the world is acquainted with Jesus, the Son of God who came to earth and lived in the flesh. But Jesus, the second member of the Trinity, existed long before He appeared on the earth. He has existed for all eternity, as the Gospel of John indicates:

In the beginning was the Word, and the Word was with God, and the Word was God. He was in the beginning with God. All things were made through Him, and without Him nothing was made that was made. In Him was life, and the life was the light of men. And the light shines in the darkness, and the darkness did not comprehend it.[5]

God's Word existed in the beginning of time. If we could see as far back as time goes, we would find that God's Word existed even before that.

The Word was working with God *and* the Word *was* God. But, how is that possible? The answer to this question is found in this divine truth: Jesus was in existence with God in the beginning—in the form of the Word.

How do we know that the "Word" spoken of in John 1:1-5 refers to Jesus? Consider the following Scriptures:

For there are three that bear witness in heaven: the Father, the Word, and the Holy Spirit; and these three are one.[6]

He was clothed with a robe dipped in blood, and His name is called The Word of God.[7]

And the Word became flesh and dwelt among us, and we beheld His glory, the glory as of the only begotten of the Father, full of grace and truth.[8]

Jesus was working with God in the beginning, and He was God. He had not yet taken on human form; He had not yet been born in Bethlehem. He had not yet died on the cross or been glorified as Christ. He was in the form of the Word.

The mystery of the Trinity is one of the greatest mysteries in the Bible. God the Father, God the Son, and God the Holy Spirit are all equal, yet they function in different ways on the earth.

In the creation of the world, all three members of the Godhead were present and active. The Bible is very specific regarding the role of the Word in all that occurred. Scripture tells us that *"all things were made through Him* [the Word]. *"*[9] Hebrews 11:3 declares, *"... The worlds were framed by the word of God, so that the things which are seen were not made of things which are visible."*

How does this role in creation relate to the topic of prayer and its power source? Very simply: without the Word of God speaking things into existence, nothing would have been created. The earth would have remained *"without form and void,"* just as Genesis 1:2 describes its condition *"in the beginning."*

We can see why it is so important for us to use God's Word in our prayers today! God Himself used the Word in the creation of the world. We must follow His example and use the Word to bring about the "creation" of His plans here on earth.

All aspects of God's will are accomplished through His Word. The Word brings life and light to men. It is the light of the world and a light to our individual paths. The Word illuminates the darkness, brings clarity to confusion, and directs us in the ways we should go.

The Word equips us for life. We were never meant to live our lives in the darkness. In the darkness, our minds, our emotions—the elements of what we call the flesh—scream for relief. In the darkness, we operate out of our own will; we are preoccupied by the flesh and do not care about the things of God. From the perspective of the darkness, our flesh knows only that it will someday die, and so it seeks the pleasures of today for temporary satisfaction.

But we do not have to live in the darkness. We are called to be children of light, people of the Word!

In John 1, Word is actually translated from the Greek word *lógos*. The word *lógos* means "the divine expression" of God."[10]

The Logos, or Word, described in this passage is Jesus, and when you pray the Word over a certain situation, you are literally "applying Jesus" to that problem or circumstance.

On the other hand, when you don't use the Word in your prayers, no matter how sincere you may be, you are not actually applying Jesus to the situation.

Additionally, speaking the written Word (Scripture) allows the Living Word (Jesus Christ) to operate in the earth. When you speak God's Word, it is infused with power, and it begins to work to accomplish God's will.

Hear me on this: learn to use God's Word in your prayers so that Jesus, the One with all of the authority and power, can move in your life and produce God's plans for you.

When Jesus Himself taught about prayer, He warned against using meaningless words: *"When you pray, do not use vain repetitions as the heathen do. For they think that they will be heard for their many words."*[11]

We must learn to make our words in prayer count! The length of our prayers means nothing if we are not praying the Word, praying effective prayers that will yield results.

The Purpose of the Word

> *All Scripture is given by inspiration of God, and is profitable for doctrine [or teaching], for reproof, for correction, for instruction in righteousness, that the man of God may be complete, thoroughly equipped for every good work.*[12]

There are many purposes for the Word of God: to teach, to reprove, to correct, to instruct, but all of these relate to the final result in the life of the believer: righteousness.

Whenever you are in doubt about what you should be doing, go to the Word. Whatever decisions you have to make, go to the Word and see what it has to say about the situations you are facing. The Word will distinguish between what is right and what is wrong.

Second Timothy 3:16 tells us that the Word is "profitable." The word *profitable* means "yielding advantageous returns or results."[13] When we pray the Word of God, we will see our prayers become effective; we will witness the advantageous results they yield. It is to our advantage to use the Word when we pray!

If you want to see any sort of positive change in your life, you must use the Word of God. You can read self-help books if you like, but the basis for change in your life should be the Bible, not self-help books.

Reading Christian books, such as the one you are holding in your hands right now, can be very helpful. Books like this one encourage your faith and teach the ways of God. Yet, these books must always be considered supplements to the highest Book, the Word of God.

- As Paul explained in his letter to Timothy, the Word is "profitable" in many ways. Let's focus on three:

- The Word *teaches* us. The word *teach* means "to impart knowledge of or skill in."[14] God's Word brings life as it imparts knowledge and gives us skills to operate in God's Kingdom.

- The Word *reproves* us. The word *reprove* means "to express disapproval of."[15] The Scriptures are the measuring stick by which we can judge our thoughts, attitudes, and behaviors. How can we know whether we are doing something wrong? Look in the Word. And how do we know whether we are doing something right? Again—look in the Word. It is the standard by which we must measure ourselves.

- The Word *trains us in righteousness.* The Bible instructs us in the ways of God, which are completely foreign to our human nature. Christians are called to live by a different set of rules from the one the world follows. The world says that it is perfectly fine to argue with your neighbors, even "cuss them out" if necessary, when they do something that angers you. But that is not a "perfectly fine" way for Christians to behave. The Scriptures say to "love your enemy" and "turn the other cheek." And that is what the Christian is called to do. How does a Christian learn to behave in godly ways? Simply by following the Word.

As we humble ourselves before the Lord and allow His Word to teach us, reprove us, correct us, and train us in righteousness, several things will begin to take place:

First, the condition of our hearts will be revealed. You may be completely unaware of an issue in your heart that God wants to address, but as you diligently meditate on His Word, go to Bible studies, go to church, and *pray* the Word, God will bring it to your attention. The Word will pinpoint the condition of your heart.

Second, our minds will be renewed. This process produces a spiritual chain reaction that leads to the fulfillment of God's will in our lives. Consider Paul's words:

And do not be conformed to this world, but be transformed by the renewing of your mind, that you may prove what is that good and acceptable and perfect will of God.[16]

Before the Fall of humankind, the minds of Adam and Eve never needed to be renewed; they were not contending with a sin nature. But since that time, we must continually battle against the carnal mind. We must continue to go to church, study the Word, and spend time in prayer, or our minds will immediately begin to slip back into natural, worldly ways of thinking. The mind must constantly be renewed, and that can only take place through the Word of God.

Third, the Word helps us to understand who God is. Without the Scriptures, it would be difficult to get to know our heavenly Father, to learn of His greatness and power—and His love. But He has provided us with His Word, an account of His dealings with humankind throughout the ages, a living testimony to His character, a way to make Himself known to us.

The Book of Psalms alone contains powerful teachings about who God is. The psalms speak of His works revealed in nature, His mighty acts of deliverance, and the history of His dealings with humanity. The psalms declare God's glory, majesty, greatness, and love for all of His creation.

Fourth, the Word is the one weapon that will keep the enemy under our feet.

Consider Jesus' response when the devil came to Him with temptation. Jesus simply said: *"It is written...."*[17] Every time He was tempted, Jesus responded with these words, and satan could not gain a foothold.

Jesus provided this as a pattern for us to use to defeat the enemy in our own lives. We are to respond saying: "It is written...."

Jesus passed His authority on to His followers: *"I give you the authority to trample on serpents and scorpions, and over all the power of the enemy, and nothing shall by any means hurt you."*[18]

When we speak the Word in the authority of the name of Jesus, satan trembles! We defeat him with the Word of God.

The Power of the Word

The Word of God is uniquely powerful; it is able to create what did not exist before, and it is mighty in bringing change to our circumstances.

For the Word of God is living and powerful, and sharper than any two-edged sword, piercing even to the division of soul and spirit, and of joints and marrow, and is a discerner of the thoughts and intents of the heart. And there is no creature hidden from His sight, but all things are naked and open to the eyes of Him to whom we must give account.[19]

This passage of Scripture brilliantly describes the dynamism of the Word. It reminds us that the Word was given with a purpose—to bring forth God's will in every life and in every situation.

The Word of God is alive. *"The Word of God is living."* In the same way that prayer is a living entity, the Word of God is alive unto itself.

As we learned from John 1, the Word *is* God; it is Jesus in Word form. As long as God is alive and seated on His throne, Jesus is alive. And if Jesus is alive, the Word of God is alive. Because it is alive and has a being and a distinct existence, it is capable of causing things to happen, of creating change upon the earth. God is purposeful regarding His Word: *"He sends out His command to the earth; His word runs very swiftly."*[20]

The Word of God is powerful. *"The Word of God is living and powerful."* God's Word is "energetically efficacious"! It has the ability to act or perform with effectiveness—it gets things done! It is a force, a cause of motion unto itself.

The power of God's Word can be most easily seen in the creation of the world. In Genesis 1, we read words like this: *"Then God said, 'Let there be...'; and there was..."* (see verses 3-24). Whatever God said *happened*.

Hebrews 11:3 declares: *"By faith we understand that the worlds were framed by the word of God, so that the things which are seen were not made of things which are visible."* We have been given the same authority in the earth, to speak forth God's Word and see results. God has invested a great deal in our ability as humans to speak. His Word says: *"Death and life are in the power of the tongue, and those who love it will eat its fruit."*[21]

The Word of God is a sharp weapon. *"The Word of God is...sharper than any two-edged sword."* The Word of God is the sword that we use to defeat the enemy. It is the weapon we use to recapture everything the devil has stolen from our lives and the lives of our family members and loved ones.

The Word can be used defensively to keep the enemy at bay. But it can also be used as an offensive weapon to destroy the enemy's plans. When we pray God's Word, it produces what God wants for us.

The Word of God separates the soul and the spirit. *"The Word of God is…sharper than any two-edged sword, piercing even to the division of soul and spirit, and of joints and marrow."* The Word will separate the carnal man (the flesh, the soul) from the spiritual man.

The Greek word for "soul" that is used here is *psuche* (psoo-khay'),[22] and it literally means "the seat of the feelings, of desire, of the affections and of aversions."[23] The *soul* contains all of our fleshly desires, affections, and emotions—the things that our hearts crave when we are not in full submission to the Lord.

In contrast, the Greek word for "spirit" is *pneuma* (pnyoo'-mah),[24] which refers to that part of man that is receptive to the Spirit of God. The Word of God is the only thing that can discern, separate, or distinguish between the carnal person and the spiritual person.

The Word of God discerns our thoughts and intentions. *"The Word of God is…a discerner of the thoughts and intents of the heart."* The Word of God is capable of judging the deepest parts of our hearts. It can discern what is going on inside a person; it is able to reveal what a person's true motives, intents, and thoughts are—even the ones they would never share with anyone else.

Put this principle to the test. If you are experiencing difficulty at your place of employment (or in your home, business, church, etc.), begin to pray the Word in that place. Go there before other people arrive or stay late after everyone has left. Speak the Word aloud in your office, home, or church. Allow the Word time to do its work of discerning the thoughts and intents of people's hearts. Watch and see what is revealed. The truth always comes out when God's Word is spoken.

The Word of God is truth. "All things are naked and open to the eyes of Him to whom we must give account." God's Word is Truth. The Greek word for "truth" is aletheia[25] which means "what is true in any matter under consideration."[26] The word true indicates, "the state of being the case of the fact."[27] Jesus prayed that we would be sanctified by God's Word, which is Truth:

> *But now I come to You, and these things I speak in the world, that they may have My joy fulfilled in themselves. I have given them Your word; and the world has hated them because they are not of the world, just as I am not of the world. I do not pray that You should take them out of the world, but that You should keep them from the evil one. They are not of the world, just as I am not of the world. Sanctify them by Your truth. Your word is truth. As You sent Me into the world, I also have sent them into the world.*[28]

To be sanctified by Truth is to become more and more Christlike and better equipped to go into the world and do God's bidding. Earlier we considered the process of sanctification from the specific perspective of renewing the mind:

> *I* [also] *beseech you, therefore, brethren, by the mercies of God, that you present your bodies a living sacrifice, holy, acceptable to God, which is your reasonable service. And do not be conformed to this world, but be transformed by the renewing of your mind, that you may prove what is that good and acceptable and perfect will of God.*[29]

The hope found in this passage from Romans is that we would be reshaped by Truth, that our minds and our prayers would be so filled with God's Word that we would be completely transformed. When that occurs, our prayers will yield amazing results for the Kingdom of God!

The Word's Job Description

In Chapter 2, "A Definition of Prayer," it was explained that the Word of God must be loaded into our prayer vehicles to successfully complete God's mission.

Just as NASA's mission is accomplished through the combined work of astronauts who perform different job descriptions, God's will is carried out through His Word, which also has multiple "job functions." Those functions are set in motion every time we load His Word into our prayers. When working in combination, these functions are able to complete the necessary work to accomplish God's mission(s) for our lives.

The Word's multiple job functions include:

1. A Navigation System: The Word of God directs and guides our prayers to the plans of God in the supernatural and brings them back to the earth. It also guides our lives in accordance with God's will and gives us direction. The Bible says: *"Your Word is a lamp to my feet and a light to my path."*[30]

2. An Irrigation System: The Word of God waters the seeds that have been sown in the form of Word-filled prayers and brings forth the intended fruit. It provides the necessary moisture for life and growth. When Ezekiel spoke God's Word to the dry bones in Ezekiel 37, his spoken word watered the bones and they began to live again.

The Bible describes the heavenly "irrigation process" this way:

For as the rain comes down, and the snow from heaven, and do not return there, but water the earth, and make it bring forth and bud, that it may give seed to the sower and bread to the eater, so shall my word be that goes forth from My mouth; it shall not return to Me void, but it shall accomplish what I please, and it shall prosper in the thing for which I sent it.[31]

3. A Support System: The Word of God provides the support necessary to build an effective prayer.

The world that we live in is framed by God's Word. This frame can be likened to the frame of a house. When a house is being built, a frame must be erected to give the house shape. The frame defines the shape of the house and supports the necessary components of the house. Without the frame, there can be no house. Sheetrock is laid on the frame, electrical wiring is laced through the frame, and plumbing is placed within the frame. The critical elements for building a house are supported by the frame.

God's Word is the key support for our existence. Every important element of life hangs on His Word. A prayer unframed by the Word of God does not yield results. Here's what the Word says about itself:

By faith we understand that the worlds were framed by the word of God, so that the things which are seen were not made of things which are visible.[32]

4. A Manufacturing System: The Word of God makes on earth what God has created in Heaven. When we speak His Word, it begins to construct the earthly manifestation of God's plans for our lives. Anything we experience on earth that reflects His Kingdom has already been formulated in Heaven. Praying God's Word connects us with His reality and makes His reality ours. The creation demonstrates this dynamic: "Then God said, 'Let there be light'; and there was light."[33]

5. A Healing Agent: The Word of God is medicine for our souls and our bodies. When we are sick, we are to speak life into the sickness using His Word. It is true that God will use doctors to bring about healing, but God's Word is what brings the cure. The Bible is clear on this:

[God] sent His Word and healed them, and delivered them from their destructions.[34]

My son, give attention to My words; incline your ear to My sayings. Do not let them depart from your eyes; keep them in the midst of your heart; for they are life to those who find them, and health to all their flesh.[35]

6. Food for Living: The Word of God is the nourishment that keeps us alive and healthy. Natural food alone will not sustain the believer. Without the spiritual nutrition of God's Word, we will die a slow death. Jesus said as much: *"It is written, 'Man shall not live by bread alone, but by every word that proceeds from the mouth of God.'"*[36]

7. A Surgical Tool: The Word of God is a double-edged sword that has the power to divide the soul from the spirit. It is able to remove or repair anything that prevents us from being perfected to do His will. The following passage bears repeating:

The Word of God is living and powerful, and sharper than any two-edged sword, piercing even to the division of soul and spirit, and of joints and marrow, and is a discerner of the thoughts and intents of the heart.[37]

8. A Weapon: The Word of God enables us to stand toe-to-toe with the devil and prevail against him. In Matthew 4:1-11, Jesus showed us how to foil the plans of the devil by using God's Word so that the Master's plan succeeds. Though tempted three times by satan, Jesus used the might of the Word to remain steadfast and to cause the tempter to flee:

[Jesus] answered and said, "It is written:' Man shall not live by bread alone, but by every word that proceeds from the mouth of God'" (verse 4).

Jesus said to him, "It is written again, 'You shall not tempt the Lord your God'" (verse 7).

*Jesus said to him, "Away with you, satan! **For it is written, 'You shall worship the Lord your God, and Him only you shall serve'"** *(verse 10).

The authority Jesus had is the authority we have—to use the Word of God. When we do, the devil will flee from us, his actions will be destroyed, and God's plans will succeed.

It is only when we pray, using God's Word, that we can truly say, "Mission accomplished!" The Bible makes this enduring promise:

So shall My word be that goes forth from My mouth; it shall not return to Me void, but it shall accomplish what I please, and it shall prosper in the thing for which I sent it.[38]

Practice Praying the Word

Before we move on in our study of prayer, this is an excellent time for you to begin to practice praying God's Word.

Below are scriptural prayer examples and exercises. The examples demonstrate how you can personalize Scriptures and pray them directly to God. The exercises are your opportunity to do the personalizing yourself.

As you read the following Scripture passages and prayers, notice how the prayers have been reworded to position you as the pray-er engaged in Word-based conversation with God.

After you have completed Exercises 1 and 2, you will be ready to open your Bible, choose a passage (the Book of Psalms is a good place to start), personalize it, and pray it back to God. (See Exercise 3.)

Make this a practice in your daily life—especially in conjunction with the principles found throughout this book. You will begin to experience more power in your prayer life and you will see better results!

Example 1: Prayer of Praise (from Psalm 97:1-6)

The following Scripture passage contains expressions of praise to God.

Scripture Passage

The Lord reigns; let the earth rejoice; let the multitude of isles be glad! Clouds and darkness surround Him; righteousness and justice are the foundation of His throne. A fire goes before Him, and burns up His enemies round about. His lightnings light the world; the earth sees and trembles. The mountains melt like wax at the presence of the Lord, at the presence of the Lord of the whole earth. The heavens declare His righteousness, and all the peoples see His glory.

Scriptural Prayer

Father, You reign; let the earth rejoice; let the multitude of the isles be glad! Clouds and darkness surround You; righteousness and justice are the foundations of Your throne. A fire goes before You, and burns up Your enemies round about. Your lightnings light the world; the earth sees and trembles. The mountains melt like wax at Your presence; at Your presence, the Lord of the whole earth. The heavens declare Your righteousness and all the peoples see Your glory. Amen.

Exercise 1: Prayer of Praise (from Psalm 95:1-5)

Read the following Scripture passage. Then proceed to the scriptural prayer and fill in the blanks to personalize it. (The first two blanks have been filled in for you.)

Scripture Passage

Oh come, let us sing to the Lord! Let us shout joyfully to the Rock of our salvation. Let us come before His presence with thanksgiving;

let us shout joyfully to Him with psalms. For the Lord is the great God, and the great King above all gods. In His hand are the deep places of the earth; the heights of the hills are His also. The sea is His, for He made it; and His hands formed the dry land.

Scriptural Prayer

Today I come to sing to You, Lord! _____ shout joyfully to the Rock of _____ salvation. _____ come before _____ presence with thanksgiving; _____ shout joyfully to _____ with psalms. For _____ are the great God and the great King above all gods. In _____ hand are the deep places of the earth; the heights of the hills are _____ also. The sea is _____, for _____ made it; and _____ hands formed the dry land.

(See Appendix A for the completed version of this prayer.)

Example 2: Prayer of Blessing for Those Who Fear the Lord (from Psalm 128)

The following Scripture passage contains promises of God for you and your loved ones.

Scripture Passage

Blessed is every one who fears the Lord, who walks in His ways. When you eat the labor of your hands, you shall be happy, and it shall be well with you. Your wife shall be like a fruitful vine in the very heart of your house, your children like olive plants all around your table. Behold, thus shall the man be blessed who fears the Lord. The Lord bless you out of Zion, and may you see the good of Jerusalem all the days of your life. Yes, may you see your children's children. Peace be upon Israel.

Scriptural Prayer

Father, I am blessed because I fear You and walk in Your ways. When I eat the labor of my hands, I shall be happy, and it shall be well with me. My spouse shall be like a fruitful vine in the very heart of my house, my children like olive plants all around my table. Behold, I shall be blessed because I fear You, Lord. Lord, bless me out of Zion, and I will see the good of Jerusalem all the days of my life. Yes, I will see my children's children. Peace be upon Israel. Amen.

Exercise 2: Biblical Confession About the Believer (from Psalm 92:12-15)

Read the following Scripture passage. Then proceed to the scriptural prayer and fill in the blanks to personalize it.

Scripture Passage

The righteous shall flourish like a palm tree, he shall grow like a cedar in Lebanon. Those who are planted in the house of the Lord shall flourish in the courts of our God. They shall still bear fruit in old age; they shall be fresh and flourishing, to declare that the Lord is upright; He is my rock, and there is no unrighteousness in Him.

Scriptural Prayer

As the righteous, _____ shall flourish like a palm tree. _____ shall grow like a cedar in Lebanon. _____ _____ planted in the house of the Lord, and _____ shall flourish in the courts of _____ God. _____ shall bear fruit in _____ old age; _____ shall be fresh (fat) and flourishing (green), and _____ _____ declare that the Lord is upright; _____ _____ my rock, and there is no unrighteousness in _____.

(See Appendix A for the completed version of this prayer.)

Exercise 3: Declaration of God's Will for Successful Living (from Psalm 1)

Now, try praying God's Word straight from your Bible. Read Psalm 1 and personalize it so that it becomes a prayer from you or a prayer for a loved one. If necessary, write out the Scripture and plug yourself into it. Pray this Scripture over your life, expecting it to accomplish God's promises for you.

After writing your scriptural prayer, compare it to the example provided in Appendix A. Please note that it is OK to articulate Scripture slightly differently from the way it is written in the Bible. It is usually necessary to change the wording somewhat in order to plug yourself into the scriptural prayer.

For example, Psalm 92:12-15 begins: *"The righteous shall flourish like a palm tree...."* Your scriptural prayer using this psalm begins, "As the righteous, I shall flourish like a palm tree." Psalm 95:1-5 starts out with *"Oh come, let us sing to the Lord!"* The scriptural prayer using this psalm starts out with "Today I come to sing to You, Lord!"

Personalize the Scripture to include yourself, but do not add, delete, or alter words that would change the context or meaning of the Scripture. I recommend that you use a Bible version that closely communicates the original meaning of Scripture. The examples and exercises in this chapter are based on the New King James Version of the Bible. However, the New Living Translation is another great version to use because it is written in contemporary language and reads closer to the way we express ourselves today.

CHAPTER 5

PRAY "THE MODEL PRAYER"—PART I

Our Father in heaven, hallowed be Your name.
Your Kingdom come, Your will be done on earth
as it is in heaven.
Give us today our daily bread.
And forgive us our debts, as we forgive our debtors.
And do not lead us into temptation,
but deliver us from the evil one.
For Yours is the Kingdom and the power
and the glory forever. Amen."—Matthew 6:9-13

The Lord's Prayer, arguably the most well-known prayer in Christendom, has been recited throughout the centuries.

The prayer is known by millions of people. It is memorized by school-aged children in Sunday school and repeated by adults during weekly worship services. Yet few realize what they are praying when they recite this prayer.

For many, the reciting of The Lord's Prayer has become a rote activity, a set of empty words that ring hollow to the believer and God. Beginning in this chapter, we will take a closer look at this prayer and discover the power of this prayerful model left to us by Jesus.

> *Now it came to pass, as He was praying in a certain place, when He ceased, that one of His disciples said to Him, "Lord, teach us to pray, as John also taught his disciples."*[1]

This is an interesting request coming from one of Jesus' disciples. They had been with Him for a while and had listened to His messages; witnessed Him perform miracles, healing, and deliverance; and watched Him pray. As Jews, they had understood the value of prayer since childhood. What, then, prompted the disciples to ask Jesus to teach them how to pray? Theologian William Barclay provides insight:

> There could be nothing more natural than that one of Jesus' disciples should come to Him and ask Him to teach them how to pray (Luke 11:1), for the Jews were characteristically and preeminently a praying people. They came to God with an absolute confidence that God desired their prayers and that God would hear. No Jew ever doubted the power of prayer. No Jew ever doubted that God's ear and heart were open to the prayer of all His children.[2]

Marvin R. Wilson, another noted theologian, speaks of the pervasiveness of prayer in the life of the Jew. Prayer was continuous because the presence of God was (and is) continuous. Because every aspect of life was touched by God, it was also touched by prayer.

In the first century church, prayer was not solely for religious activities, but was included in all walks and ways of life. Prayer was said by the farmer for the tilling of the soil, by the baker for the making of the bread, by the merchant for the selling of his wares. Prayer was recited "upon hearing bad news and good news, when smelling fragrant plants, and when eating food or drinking wine. A Jew offered a prayer in the presence of thunder, lightning, rainbows, and comets."[3]

According to Wilson, prayer was to be offered for and about everything that touched a person's life. Prayer was even offered to bless God for the ability to urinate. For this basic function of life one would say:

> Blessed is He who has formed man in wisdom and created in him many orifices and many cavities. It is fully known before the throne of Thy glory that if one of them should be [improperly] opened or one of them closed it would be impossible for a man to stand before Thee.[4]

As Jews, prayer was an integral part of life for the disciples. What I don't want you to miss is that the disciples asked Jesus to teach them how to pray, which suggests that prayer is not something we are born knowing how to do; prayer is learned behavior. It is to be taught.

Like reading and writing, prayer requires some education and training. Jesus' disciples had been accustomed to prayer, and the idea of being taught to pray was not unheard of.

Yet there must have been something about Jesus' prayer life that caused the disciples to question Him. No doubt, when He prayed, things happened. And so they asked Him to teach them how to do what He was doing. He answered them by providing "The Model Prayer," a detailed way to pray effectively:

> *In this manner, therefore, pray: Our Father in heaven, hallowed be Your name. Your Kingdom come. Your will be done on earth as it is in heaven. Give us this day our daily bread. And forgive us our debts, as we forgive our debtors. And do not lead us into temptation, but deliver us from the evil one. For Yours is the kingdom and the power and the glory forever. Amen.*[5]

Some reading this book have a prayer life and have been praying for a long time. Perhaps someone significant in your life taught you how to pray. Maybe your family prayed together from your earliest memory. At your place of worship, you prayed. You may have even taken prayer classes or served on a prayer team. In short, prayer has been a part of your culture, and no doubt you have gotten results. Praise God!

This book is not designed to tell you that you have been praying incorrectly, but to help you strengthen your prayer life and to maximize the results of your prayers.

Why Use "The Model Prayer"?

The question may be asked, "Why should we use this prayer model?" Well, consider the following reasons:

1. Jesus said it. Jesus presented this model and told us, His disciples, to use it. When asked by His followers how to pray, He told them what to pray and instructed them not to pray like the religious people of their day who prayed prayers filled with meaningless words.[6] Jesus did not give options, but He presented one prayer for all believers regardless of background or experience. During my study of Scripture, I have not found another model of prayer recommended by Jesus. There are many prayers spoken by different people in the Bible such as Paul, Samuel, Hannah, and David. Yet Jesus did not respond to His disciples by reciting their prayers; instead, He proffered a set of words that He wanted them to use. I like to call His example "The Model Prayer" or "The Kingdom Prayer." It is different in its focus and content, and it contains a wealth of revelation that will forever transform humanity. Since Jesus presented this model, it should be of the utmost importance and the Body of Christ should pay attention to it and incorporate it into their daily living.

2. It is God-centered. The Model Prayer helps our prayers to be God-centered instead of self-centered. When we pray according to Jesus' example, we ask for God's Kingdom to come on earth *before* we ask Him to meet our own needs and desires.

3. It is productive. God's ways are perfect; therefore, God's model for praying will produce more of His results for our lives. This prayer has been *designed* to maximize our results.

4. It is scriptural.

5. It is strategic. The Model Prayer offers a balanced strategy for praying.

6. It is practical. Once you begin to practice the model, it becomes second nature.

7. It is transformational. Because the prayer focuses on God's will, it works to transform you. As you pray according to the model, your life will change. You will see it unfold and change according to God's design and specifications.

8. It is exciting. Your prayer life will become more meaningful and exciting as you work with God to pray for His interests.

9. It is intimate. Because this prayer is God-centered, you will enjoy a new and fresh awareness of God the Father, the Son, and the Holy Spirit.

10. It is the living Word. You will experience the power, presence, and providence of God because of the repeated use of His Word. As you speak His Word to retrieve His plans, that same Word will work in you to produce His will for your individual life.

11. It produces faith. Your faith in and dependence on God will increase as you learn how to partner with Him and follow the order of The Model Prayer.

12. It is relational. Your relationship with God will grow and mature as you learn to follow His lead while praying through The Model Prayer pattern. Additionally, as you pray God's Word using The Model Prayer as a template, His Word will teach you about His character and actions.

13. It is broadly applicable. This model can be applied to your personal and professional life.

14. It is powerful. As you pray for God's Kingdom to be established, you will become a powerful change agent for your family, business, community, and nation.

15. It brings glory to God. The Model Prayer glorifies God, both in its praise for Him and through the results it yields.

16. It exalts Jesus.

17. It magnifies the Holy Spirit.

18. It defeats darkness. As you pray for God's will to be done, the works of the devil will be defeated.

19. It works! Anything that God creates is, by nature, effective. (Chapter 10, "Prayer and Results," presents personal testimonies of some of the results experienced by incorporating Jesus' model of prayer.)

As Jesus' modern-day disciples, we have the same opportunity to benefit from His teachings. The Model Prayer, as we have come to know it, gives us a pattern for prayer that we can use right now to accomplish God's purposes in our time.

The Six Sections of The Model Prayer

Jesus gave us the specific instructions we would need in order to pray "effective, fervent prayers."[7] The Model Prayer He gave us is relatively short, yet it contains six powerful sections the Lord wants us to use as we communicate with Him.

Each section of The Model Prayer found in Matthew 6 is vital to producing God's plans in the earth, because each covers a different area of concern. Let's identify the six sections:

Section 1: Intimate Praise and Worship

"Our Father in Heaven, hallowed be Your name" (verse 9).

Section 2: Praying God's Will

"Your kingdom come. Your will be done on earth as it is in heaven" (verse 10).

Section 3: Praying for Your Needs

"Give us this day our daily bread" (verse 11).

Section 4: Praying for Forgiveness

"And forgive us our debts, as we forgive our debtors" (verse 12).

Section 5: Praying for Protection

"And do not lead us into temptation, but deliver us from the evil one" (verse 13a).

Section 6: Kingdom Praise and Worship

"For Yours is the kingdom and the power and the glory forever. Amen" (verse 13b).

Using this six-section model doesn't dictate the length of our prayers. Using this model puts us in alignment with God's prayer program and ensures that we cover everything that God is concerned about in our prayer sessions.

Before we look at each section specifically, I have a question for you: why do you think the sections are presented in the following order?

Intimate Praise and Worship
Praying God's Will
Praying for Your Needs
Praying for Forgiveness
Praying for Protection
Kingdom Praise and Worship

As we consider these individual prayer "nuggets," we can see that they comprise a pattern of prayer. This pattern has a purpose: it helps us to focus our prayers in an ordered manner that makes our prayers more productive.

First, our praying must begin and end with giving God praise. Second, instead of immediately asking God for something, we are to speak to Him about His will. By doing this, our prayers become God-centered instead of self-centered; therefore, we become focused on what God wants to fulfill in the earth instead of on our own desires and complaints. The Model Prayer helps us to make God the center of our prayer life instead of ourselves.

I have heard many prayers over the years. Most of them began with praising God, however briefly. Yet, immediately following the praise, a petition was offered up.

I want to encourage you to listen to your prayers and the prayers of others and notice how quickly we tend to ask God to do or provide something. I do not mean to criticize; all of us have prayed to the best of our ability. Remember, most of us have had no classes on prayer, so we've learned how to pray the best way we could.

The fact remains that The Model Prayer shows that praying God's will (or His business, as I like to say) is the second most important matter in prayer. It is only after we have prayed His will that we are to make our requests.

What is most compelling about this model is the fact that asking for forgiveness is only the fourth priority on the list. I think this is phenomenal. You would think that God would require His people to take care of the sin in their lives before they could have a conversation with Him. Yet, The Model Prayer suggests otherwise.

We have all heard prayers that begin by asking God to forgive sins in hopes that this would clean up the pray-er and make him or her worthy to talk with the Lord. Well, I have good news! Through Jesus' resurrection and ascension, we are forgiven, and we are made worthy to address our heavenly Father. We have been given the legal right to be called God's children, and we are considered His righteousness. *"Let us therefore come boldly to the throne of grace...."*[8]

Daily, God waits to talk and commune with us. God looks forward to meeting with us every day. Forgiveness and repentance are important to God, but not so important that they are the first things He wants to hear from us. If that were the case, the order of the model would be different.

Furthermore, The Model Prayer makes it clear that God is the central focus of prayer. To ask Him to forgive us at the beginning of our conversation with Him would be to take the focus off of God and to put it right back on us.

Finally, this model shows us how interested God is in His people. He really is interested in having a relationship with us. He really wants to spend time with us. He is truly merciful and full of grace. He doesn't look down on us or see us as the scourge of the earth.

Notice that you can have a conversation with the Lord for hours by praising Him, attending to His business, and presenting petitions to Him before you ever address sin in your life. What a wonderful God we serve! He loves us so much that He allows us to talk and commune with Him while sin is in our lives—and He loves us enough that He will not let us leave His presence before addressing that sin. Before we end our prayer, we must address our sin. First John 1:9 assures us that, *"…He is faithful and just to forgive us our sins…."* What a relief to know that God wants to hear from us no matter the condition we may be in.

Earlier, I posed the question, "Why are the sections listed in the order that they are?" Although I've already offered several reasons for the order of the sections, I don't pretend to know all that God had in mind. Nor do the Scriptures speak directly to this specific question. However, we do know that God is a God of order. Therefore, it is important for us to regard the order He established in His model for prayer.

Another question arises about using a pattern for prayer: how can we really pray from our hearts if we have to apply a set order to our prayer? What about spontaneity? This model provides loads of opportunity for spontaneity and heartfelt expression. At the same time, it provides an order for expressing the spontaneity.

Remember, prayer is *God's* vehicle that we are to use to communicate with Him and for Him so that we can accomplish His mission on earth. Praying the way that Jesus taught the first disciples is not designed to suppress our relationship with the Father, but to build it.

It is not unusual for people to struggle initially with applying a pattern to their prayers. It takes practice, but the rewards are great. I have found, as has the team of people who have helped me teach The Model Prayer over the years, that using this model decreases my number of prayer requests. The model keeps my prayers centered on God;

therefore, my daily communications are focused on what God wants for me, my family, my church, and my community. As stated in Matthew 6:33: *"Seek first the kingdom of God and His righteousness, and all these things shall be added to you."*

This model is amazing. It contains every component needed for powerful praying and successful living. When we apply the pattern, we don't have to ask God about our wants and needs as often. We discover that our interest in His desires produces a wonderful benefit: it takes care of our needs.

This is where true communication with God begins. It is the place in prayer where we can clearly see what we ought to ask of Him so that His wonders can be performed—in our lives and our world!

Praying using The Lord's Prayer as the pattern will literally transform your life. This one short prayer will change the way you see things, the way you approach God, and the way you work with Him. Now let's study the prayer, section by section.

Section 1: Intimate Praise and Worship

Our Father in heaven, hallowed be Your name.

The Model Prayer's first line and initial section of praise and worship establishes our relationship with the Lord and sets the appropriate tone for prayer. There are three things to remember and apply as we begin to pray: first, we must acknowledge Him as Father; second, we are to offer Him thanksgiving; and third, we are to give Him adoration and praise.

1. Acknowledge God as Father. The beginning section of praise and worship is about our relationship with God. Jesus said to begin our prayer with the words *Our Father*, suggesting that God who is Father to Jesus is also our Father. God decided in advance to adopt us into His own family by bringing us to Himself through Jesus Christ. This is what He wanted to do, and it gave Him great pleasure.[9]

If Jesus said that God is our Father, then we must be God's children. The Bible tells us that we should relate to God as children, for we have a legal right to be called His children.[10] So we are to boldly go before Him, not as strangers, but as children of the promise.[11] Psalm 100:3 says: *"Know that the Lord, He is God; It is He who has made us, and not we ourselves...."*

The Lord our God, the One who made us, loves us with an unconditional love. If you have children, you have an idea of the kind of love that exists between a parent and a child. You want your child to know that, no matter what she does, you love her so much that she can come to you and tell you about it. You want her to know that your love for her cannot be diminished, no matter the circumstances. But, in order for her to come to you unflinchingly, she has to feel nurtured, approved, affirmed, and protected.

As human parents, with high (or low) expectations and stress-filled lives, we sometimes find it difficult to maintain our loving relationships with our children. On the flip side, as children of human parents, we can also find it hard to relate to God as Father, particularly if we had troublesome relationships with our earthly parents.

Most of us project our past family experiences onto God. If we had parents who were strict and hard to please, that is how we see God. We could not please them, so how can we please God? Perhaps we grew up in a home where we were physically or emotionally abused. It is hard to trust a parent who deliberately hurts us. As a result, we may see God, not as a Father who loves us unconditionally, but as a Father who is out to harm us.

Thank God for His redeeming power. He can wipe away those hurtful memories. He can address the wounds that we are still carrying around from childhood. He can change our perspectives about what a parent can and should be like. He can heal us, if we will let Him.

Many of us had and have wonderful relationships with our parents. Therefore, it is not difficult to have a healthy, nurturing relationship with God. Regardless of your experience with your parents, you can rest assured that God's parental love is better.

As a good Father, God expects us to come to Him with soft hearts and no hesitation, comfortable in telling Him anything. "Father, I said something I shouldn't have said this morning." "Father, I had an ugly thought about someone this afternoon." "Father, I need help raising my children." "Father, I rebelled against You today." "Father, I don't always understand You or Your Kingdom." No matter what issues we take to Him, we know that He will be patient, understanding and loving—today, tomorrow, forever.

2. Offer God thanksgiving. "*Enter into His gates with thanksgiving,*" the psalmist instructs us in Psalm 100:4, "*...be thankful to Him and bless His name.*"

To gain access to an earthly king, there is a protocol: you don't just walk up to the king because you desire an audience with him. There is a path you must take. If, as is true in America, your government is not a monarchy, you may not know how to approach a king. But, thanks to the Word, the way to the Lord is common knowledge.

Kings reside and preside in palaces that have gates or doors that lead to courts, usually of different levels, that lead to the throne room. Through Jesus Christ, God resides in our hearts. *We* are His temple, and we have unlimited access to the throne room.

At any time of the day or night, we can approach God. But, we must approach Him with an attitude of thanksgiving. *"Enter into His gates with thanksgiving."* We should not just "pop in" without acknowledging His faithfulness and kingship. God wants to hear our gratitude and appreciation. *"In everything,"* Philippians 4:6 states, *"...by prayer and supplication, **with thanksgiving**, let your requests be made known to God."*

Thanksgiving is considered one of the sacrifices we are to offer to the Lord. The following Scriptures tell us so:

And when you offer a sacrifice of thanksgiving to the Lord, offer it of your own free will.[12]

I will wash my hands in innocence; so I will go about Your altar, O Lord, that I may proclaim with the voice of thanksgiving, and tell of all Your wondrous works.[13]

Offer to God thanksgiving, and pay your vows to the Most High.[14]

Let us come before His presence with thanksgiving; let us shout joyfully to Him with psalms.[15]

Let them sacrifice the sacrifices of thanksgiving, and declare His works with rejoicing.[16]

God is always ready to receive us. We must always be ready to move toward His presence with thankfulness, in the way that He has decreed.

What should we thank God for? Everything! Every day of your life you should find more and more things for which to thank God: the food on your table, the clothes in your closet, your family and friends, a good night's rest, even an unsolicited "Hello" from a stranger. God loves it when you acknowledge His goodness.

How do we thank the Lord? Specifically. "Thank You, Lord, for a good day at work." "Thank You for blessing the children on their school projects." "Thank You for helping me to deliver that speech today." "Thank You for helping us to come home safely through the rainstorm." "Thank You for helping me to forgive my spouse." "Thank You for getting me out of that jam."

When I come before the Lord, I see a picture in my mind. I see myself entering the throne room of Heaven and walking before the Father. He's my Daddy, and His arms are stretched out toward me; His expression is welcoming, and I can feel His love. I see myself crawl into His lap and lean upon His bosom. He's not a big, bad God sitting up high in the heavens with a huge, intimidating crown on His head and a sword by His side, ready to cut off my head. No; He's my Daddy, the One whom I trust with all of my heart, and I am about to go talk to Him!

Because I know Him, I know that He likes to hear me thank Him for all of the kindness He demonstrates toward me, the blessings He bestows upon me, and the good gifts He gives to me. And so, I begin to speak: "Father, I thank You for Your blessings. I thank You for excellent health and enduring strength. Thank You for taking care of my children and husband and meeting all our needs. Thank You for protecting us from evil and destroying wicked assignments against us. Thank You for giving me wisdom and knowledge to lead my staff. Thank You for helping me to give an excellent presentation. Thank You for helping me to produce results that benefit my company and community. Thank You, thank You, thank You, Lord, for who You are and what You are doing in my life."

I encourage you, before you read any further, to take a moment and reflect over the last 24 to 48 hours. Consider all that God has done or given during that span of time. I use the 24- to 48-hour timeframe because it keeps me sensitive to what God is doing in my life every day. I become more aware of His presence, and I love noticing what He is doing in my life daily. Furthermore, my immediate thanksgiving shows Him that I am paying attention to His goodness and faithfulness; I am noticing Him and His works, and I am grateful and appreciative.

For the next few minutes, consider ten things for which you are thankful and list them in the blanks below. Be very detailed with your expressions of thanksgiving. Being specific with our thanks to God lets Him know that we remember what He has done for us, and it honors Him as the Source of our supply.

1.

2.

3.

4.

5.

6.

7.

8.

9.

10.

If you had to really think hard about what to thank God for, then I suggest that you practice thanking God every time you pray. This will help you to become more aware of what the Lord is doing in your life. Keep your list handy, and keep adding to it as the Holy Spirit brings things to your mind. Use that list in your prayer time as you "enter into His gates with thanksgiving." Gratitude is a perfect state to be in as we begin to praise Him.

3. Offer God adoration and praise. God is holy; therefore, we say, *"Hallowed be thy name."* As we approach God's throne room, Psalm 100:4 instructs us to come into His courts with praise. When we praise Him, we extol His character and His works.

Many times our prayers are laced with praise instead of saturated with praise. Often, we give God a brief acknowledgement and then spend the rest of the prayer asking Him for something, lamenting about our frailties, or telling Him what needs to be done.

It is not that God needs our praise, but our praise blesses Him and speaks to the earth about His goodness. David says in Psalm 34:1, *"I will bless the Lord at all times; His praise shall continually be in my mouth."* David also wrote, *"Praise from the upright is beautiful."*[17] When we pray, we should spend time blessing God and speaking of His mighty works.

We know that Jesus instructed the disciples to say *"Hallowed be thy name."* According to William Barclay, author of *The Lord's Prayer*, the word *hallow* was translated from the Greek word, *hagiazein*, which means "to hold sacred or treat as holy."[18] Barclay explains further:

> But what does that mean? We can best come at this from remembering the meaning of "hagios." "Hagios" is the adjective meaning holy; but the basic idea behind it is the idea of difference. That which is "hagios" is different from ordinary things; it belongs to a different sphere of quality and of being. That is why God is supremely The Holy One, for God supremely belongs to a different sphere of life and being. This meaning becomes even clearer when we examine the word in use. The commandment is to remember the Sabbath day to keep it holy (Exodus 20:8). That is to say, the Sabbath day is to be regarded and to be kept as different from other days. The instruction to consecrate the priest (Leviticus 21:8). This also is the word "hagiazein", and clearly the meaning is to set the priest apart so that he is different from others and from ordinary men, so that, we might now say, he is different from laymen.

> When we arrive at this stage, we can see that the meaning of the word "hagiazein" is beginning to acquire the meaning of

reverence, for reverence is the characteristic attitude to that which is different, that which belongs to a sphere of being other than our own. So, then, we arrive at the conclusion that "to hallow" means to reverence.[19]

The Scriptures tell us to treat God's name as holy and sacred. When we pray, we must first reverence the name of God with honor and adulation. He is the King of kings, and He must be treated as such. Oftentimes believers treat God as if He is a mere mortal. But He is not mortal; He is the Almighty God and the only living God who created all things. The Creator must be venerated by the creation.

Now, let's turn our attention to the word *name.*

In biblical times the "name" stood for much more than the name by which a person is called in the modern sense of the term. The name stood for the whole character of the person as it was known, manifested, or revealed. As Origen puts it in commenting on this petition of the Lord's Prayer, "name is a term, which summarizes and manifests the personal character of him who is named. The name stands for the 'personal and incommunicable character' of the person. The name of God, therefore, stands for the nature and the character and the personality of God as they have been revealed to men." This becomes quite clear when we see the way in which the "Name" is used in Scripture. The Psalmist (Psalm 9:10) says, 'Those who know thy name put their trust in thee.' That clearly does not mean that those who know God's name in the English sense of the term will willingly trust him; it means that those who know the character and nature and personality of God, those who know what God is like as he has revealed himself to be, will willingly trust in him."[20]

To pray *"hallowed be thy name,"* means "May you be given that unique reverence which your character and nature and personality, as you have revealed them to us, demand. To hallow God's name is to give God the reverence, the honour, the glory, the praise, the exaltation which his character demands. Calvin puts it this way: That God's name would be hallowed is nothing other than to say that God should have His own honour, of which He is worthy, so that men should never think or speak of Him without the greatest veneration.'"[21]

When we pray, we should spend time honoring God's name through praise and adoration. Don't be in a hurry. Take the time to speak highly of our Lord and Savior and to lift up the name of Jesus.

When praising God, use what the Word already says about the Lord. The Book of Psalms is the perfect book for praising and honoring God. Using His Word gives us confidence when we pray, and more importantly, it puts us in a position to bless Him. There are numerous praise and worship Scriptures we can use to pray to God. Here are a few:

Psalm 95:3-5 says:

For the Lord is the great God, and the great King above all gods. In His hand are the deep places of the earth; the heights of the hills are His also. The sea is His, for He made it; and His hands formed the dry land.

We pray:

Lord, You are a great God, and the great King above all gods. In Your hands are the deep places of the earth; the heights of the hills are Yours also. The sea belongs to You, for You made it; and Your hands formed the dry land.

Psalm 99:1-3 says:

The Lord reigns; let the peoples tremble! He dwells between the cherubim; let the earth be moved! The Lord is great in Zion, and He is high above all the peoples. Let them praise Your great and awesome name—He is holy.

We pray:

Lord, You reign! Let the peoples tremble! You dwell between the cherubim. Let the earth be moved! You are great in Zion, and You are high above all the peoples. Let them praise Your great and awesome name—You are holy!

Psalm 33:6-9 (NLT) says:

The Lord merely spoke, and the heavens were created. He breathed the word, and all the stars were born. He assigned the sea its boundaries and locked the oceans in vast reservoirs. Let the whole world fear the Lord, and let everyone stand in awe of Him. For when He spoke, the world began! It appeared at His command.

We pray:

Lord, You merely spoke and the heavens were created. You breathed the word, and all the stars were born. You assigned the sea its boundaries and locked the oceans in vast reservoirs. Let the whole world fear You, Lord, and let everyone stand in awe of You. For when You spoke, the world began! It appeared at Your command.

Lastly, when you praise God, open your mouth and speak up. Praise requires vocals. *"Make a joyful shout to the Lord, all you lands! Serve the Lord with gladness; come before His presence with singing."*[22] It sounds like a party, doesn't it? It is a party! The guest of honor, through

His Word, tells us exactly how to get the party started for Him. Shouting, serving, and singing with joy and gladness cannot be done with our mouths closed.

Imagine the following scenario: there is someone who you think very highly of, someone whose sharp dressing you wish to compliment or whose actions you wish to praise. However, before you express your feelings to this individual, you vow not to open your mouth, make any sound, use any facial expressions, or make any hand motions. As a result, your affirming words are expressed only in your own head.

When your laudatory thoughts are finished, you ask this person to respond to your praise. He looks at you quizzically, wondering what you are talking about.

Why? The reason is simple: the person that you feel so highly about was unable to enjoy your praise because he never heard it.

God wants to hear your praises. The earth needs to hear your praises. The devil and his demonic powers need to hear your praises.

Did you know that the praises of God's people wreck the devil's communications? Ephesians 2:2 identifies the devil as the *"prince of the power of the air."* That means that he has dominion over any medium that travels through air, including air and sound waves. How do we receive most of our communications? Through air and sound waves.

Have you ever wondered why there is so much trash on radio and television? Well, the controller of the frequencies that are used by radio and television is the devil. When the body of Christ lifts up praises to the Lord, we literally interrupt the air and sound waves in the earth and wreck the communications of the devil. Come on, lift up your voice and praise the Lord!

In the following exercise, practice praising God using words that He loves to hear. Read the Scripture of praise that is provided and then compose a scriptural prayer of praise by filling in the blanks. Pray this prayer out loud and enjoy the sweetness of God's Word while blessing Him with yours.

Exercise 1: Prayer of Praise (from Psalm 111:2-7 NLT)

Scripture Passage

How amazing are the deeds of the Lord! All who delight in Him should ponder them. Everything He does reveals His glory and majesty. His righteousness never fails. He causes us to remember His wonderful works. How gracious and merciful is our Lord! He gives food to those who fear Him; He always remembers His covenant. He has shown His great power to His people by giving them the lands of other nations. All He does is just and good, and all His commandments are trustworthy.

Scriptural Prayer

Father, _____ deeds are amazing! All who delight in _____ should ponder them. Everything _____ do reveals _____ glory and majesty. _____ righteousness never fails. _____ cause us to remember _____ wonderful works. _____ are gracious and merciful. _____ give food to those of us who fear _____; _____ always remember _____ covenant. _____ have shown _____ great power to _____ people by giving them the lands of other nations. All _____ do is just and good and all _____ commandments are trustworthy.

(See Appendix B for the completed version of this prayer.)

It may take some practice to use God's Word to speak to Him and to say it aloud, particularly for those of us who are used to praying only in our heads. It can feel awkward to go from inward to outward praise, whether you are by yourself or in a crowd.

In Appendix C, you will find a list of scriptural prayers of praise and worship. They will help you to practice using God's Word when you praise Him. I encourage you to activate those scriptural prayers in your prayer time with the Lord, at your place of worship, or wherever and whenever you want to honor God. It is a "cheat sheet" sanctioned by the Lord. Come out of your comfort zone, pull out your list, and use it to the glory of God.

Psalm 100 ends by saying: *"For the Lord is good; His mercy is everlasting, and His truth endures to all generations."*

Praise not only gives our awesome and merciful and eternal God the honor due Him, it also opens our hearts and prepares us to hear Him so that we can do His will.

CHAPTER 6

PRAY "THE MODEL PRAYER"—PART II

In Section 1 of The Model Prayer, we acknowledge the preciousness of our relationship with the Father as we honor Him with our praise and worship. In Section 2, we'll continue our conversation with the Father, delving into the partnership that our relationship inspires.

Section 2: Praying God's Will

> *Your kingdom come. Your will be done on earth as it*
> *is in heaven.*

The way we begin our conversation with God in Section 2 should reflect our willingness to submit to His service, seek His will, and implement His plans.

In praying God's will, our partnership with Him is what becomes most important. Instead of telling Him what needs to happen, we ought to ask Him: "Father, what do You want to talk about? What is on Your mind? What do I need to say in order for Your will to be accomplished in the earth today?"

If you will remember, Chapter 2 talked about God's partnership with us. God has chosen to partner with human beings to accomplish His plans. For some, this may be hard to imagine: to think that Almighty God, Creator of the heavens and the earth, would want to work with mere mortals. It is beyond the imagination, yet it is true. Since the beginning of time, God has desired to work with humanity.

Partnerships are mentioned throughout the Bible. God created Adam and Eve to be companions to Him and to watch over His creation.[1] God worked with Abraham to establish a people for Himself.[2] He worked with Moses to bring liberation to the Israelites.[3] He partnered with Deborah, an Israelite judge, to defeat Israel's enemies.[4] He partnered with David to establish His throne on the earth.[5] He partnered with Solomon to build a temple where He could dwell among His people.[6] He partnered with Mary to bring Jesus into the world,[7] and He partnered with His only begotten Son to bring salvation to all people.[8]

In John 4:31-33, the disciples wanted to be sure that Jesus had eaten. In verse 34, Jesus responded by saying *"My food is to do the will of Him who sent Me, and to finish His work."* Jesus embodied the perfect example of working with God to accomplish His will for humankind.

God has always been in the partnering business, and He continues to partner with us today. One of His chief partnerships involves prayer; He needs us to work with Him so that His Word is released into the supernatural and the earth.

We are God's "voice," and unless we speak up through prayer, He cannot accomplish His work. His work is manifested in the earth by His Word, and His Word has to be audibly spoken. We are the mouthpiece that speaks for Him.

When we allow our voices to be used for God's purposes, the Bible promises us a tremendous benefit:

Now this is the confidence that we have in Him, that if we ask anything according to His will, He hears us. And if we know that He hears us, whatever we ask, we know that we have the petitions that we have asked of Him.[9]

If we ask. The Lord says to ask. *Ask* doesn't just mean to petition Him. In the Greek, it means to "require," "to call for," or even "to desire."[10] As believers, we have the legal right to require, call for, or desire God's will to be manifested in the earth.

Some may frown upon the idea of putting a demand on God's Word. But Ephesians 5:1 states, *"Therefore be imitators of God as dear children."* As His children, we should follow God's example demonstrated in Psalm 33:6. *"By the word of the Lord the heavens were made and all the host of them by the breath of His mouth."* Speak God's Word in your prayers and watch God's plans become your earthly reality.

According to His will. What is God's will? God's will is His Word. Pray His Word and you'll know what He wants to accomplish on the earth and in your life.

Are you living each day as if you are in a holding pattern? I have good news for you. Your struggle will stop when you pray the Word. You will learn everything you need to know about what God wants for your life. In fact, as you live out the Word, it will custom-tailor your life.

This is how it works. The Bible doesn't say whether or not you should live at 777 Oak Lane, in a nice home surrounded by a white picket fence, with a red sports car parked in the garage. But it does say that, if you seek first the Kingdom of God, all of the things that you need will be added to you.[11]

Our wholehearted focus on Him brings the desires of our hearts to fruition. Pray and live out God's Word, and it will create the details for your life.

He will hear us. We needn't doubt whether God is listening to us, as long as we ask, require, call for, or desire what He has already told us to seek. It is a simple process:

Pray God's Word.

↓

↓→→→ (Because you prayed His Word)

↓

Know that God hears you.

↓

↓→→→ (Because you know that God heard you)

↓

Expect the Answer.

From the Lord's perspective, the children who take care of His business will have their business taken care of by Him. Therefore, results-driven prayer begins with God's Word.

The more you pray God's Word, the less asking you will need to do. According to Isaiah 65, those who are focused on God's business—His "servants" (verse 13)—will have their prayers answered, even before they can formulate their requests (verse 24).

When your prayers are centered on God's will, not only will your request list get shorter, but the Lord will bless you in ways that you cannot imagine. Still, the focus must remain on what it is that He wants to do. When we yield to God and ask Him what we should pray for, He puts His concerns on our hearts. At that point, our response should be to go to His Word and find the Scriptures related to His requests.

If the Lord wants you to pray about a particular school in your community, seek what the Word says about education and call for His will to be done by His Word.

If He wants you to pray about your neighbor down the street who may be ill, go find the appropriate Scriptures and require healing to manifest in his body.

He may direct you to pray for your boss or mayor or president. You may not be fond of any of those people, their policies, or their actions, yet the Bible says to pray for those who have rule over us so that our lives will be peaceful.[12] We are to pray for our leaders particularly when we disagree with them, believing that our prayers will put the right people in the right places to do what God wants rather than what we want.

Let's practice attending to God's business by declaring God's Word. In the following example, read the Scripture passage that is provided and develop a scriptural prayer by filling in the blanks in the paragraph that follows.

Exercise 1: Prayer of Blessings for the Family (from Psalm 128)

Scripture Passage

Blessed is every one who fears the Lord, who walks in His ways. When you eat the labor of your hands, you shall be happy and it shall be well with you. Your wife shall be like a fruitful vine in the very heart of your house, your children like olive plants all around your table. Behold, thus shall the man be blessed who fears the Lord. May the Lord bless you out of Zion, and may you see the good of Jerusalem all the days of your life. Yes, may you see your children's children. Peace be upon Israel!

Scriptural Prayer

_____ _____ *blessed because* _____ *fear the Lord and walk in His ways. When* _____ *eat the labor of* _____ *hands,* _____ *shall be happy and it shall be well with* _____. _____ _____ *shall be like a fruitful vine in the very heart of* _____ *house,* _____ *children will be like olive plants all around* _____ *table. Behold,* _____ _____ *be blessed because* _____ *fear the Lord. Lord, bless* _____ *out of Zion, and* _____ *will see the good of Jerusalem all the days of* _____ *life. Yes,* _____ *will see* _____ *children's children. Peace be upon Israel. Amen.*

(See Appendix B for the completed version of this prayer. Please note: Appendix D contains more exercises for practice.)

Tips for Scriptural Pray-ers

Before we move on to the third section of The Model Prayer, let's take a moment to consider a few helpful tips about using His Word as we pray. Both beginning and experienced pray-ers will find these hints useful.

- **Use a Bible version that is translated as close to the original text as possible so you can understand exactly what the initial writer meant.**

The New King James version is an excellent Bible for study. The New Living Translation, (another translation that is considered closely translated from the original text) is effective for praying the Word over your life because it is written in modern language. A parallel Bible that contains the New King James Version and the New Living Translation will be helpful to developing your prayers. Any of these Bibles can be found in Christian bookstores.

- **Use a concordance for help finding Scriptures.**

Most of us are not Bible scholars, and the Lord does not expect us to know the location of every Scripture. He does expect us, however, to know how to get there. The majority of Bibles have a concordance in the back, typically arranged alphabetically by words or topics under which relevant Scriptures are listed. *Strong's Concordance* is one of the most well-known resources of this type.

If you want to pray for a child, locate the heading "child" or "children." The Scriptures listed will all have the word "child" or "children" in them. Identify the Scripture that is most closely related to the topic you want to pray about.

For example, your prayer topic may be for the future of a child; you will find Proverbs 22:6, which states: *"Train up a child in the way he should go, and when he is old he will not depart from it."* Your scriptural prayer might be, "Lord, because I am training up my child in the way she should go, when she is old she will not depart from it."

- **Use other faith-based books as references.**

There are several books on the market and in your library designed to help pray-ers use God's Word. Author Lee Roberts has written a series of books about praying God's will that conveniently categorize Scriptures. *Prayers That Avail Much*, by Germaine Copeland, converts Scriptures into prayer form and is also a source for Bible information.

- **Use commentaries to aid your understanding of Scripture passages.**

A commentary contains interpretations of Scripture. Written by different authors, commentaries are helpful to understanding the meaning of Scripture. They will help you to pray using Scriptures in their proper context.

- **Read the verses of Scripture that precede and follow the Scripture passage you have selected.**

Reading adjacent verses ensures that your chosen Scripture is appropriate to your topic and prayed in its proper context. Let's assume that you have decided to pray for favor. You look in the concordance for "favor" and among the Scriptures listed is Proverbs 3:4, which states: *"And so find favor and high esteem in the sight of God and man."*

You then pray, "Father, I confess that I will find favor and high esteem with You and man." However, there is a condition to finding favor in the preceding verse. Proverbs 3:3 states: *"Let not mercy and truth forsake you; bind them around your neck, write them on the tablet of your heart."*

So, in order to find favor with God and man, we must bind mercy and truth around our necks. In other words, if we make mercy and truth part of our lifestyle, we will receive favor and be highly esteemed.

Now, having the complete thought in mind, your prayer is, "Father, I will not let mercy and truth forsake me. I bind them around my neck and write them on the tablet of my heart. Therefore, I expect to have favor and high esteem with You and people."

- **Be aware that "if, then" Scriptures carry conditions that must be met.**

Malachi 3:10-12 provides an example.

"Bring all the tithes into the storehouse, that there may be food in My house, and try Me now in this," says the Lord of hosts, "If I will not open for you the windows of heaven and pour out for you such blessing that there will not be room enough to receive it. And I will rebuke the devourer for your sakes, so that he will not destroy the fruit of your ground, nor shall the vine fail to bear fruit for you in the field," says the Lord of hosts; "And all nations will call you blessed, for you will be a delightful land," says the Lord of hosts.

In order to pray Malachi 3:10-12, you must first answer the question, *Am I a tither?* If you are a tither, then you can pray, "Father, I have brought all of my tithes into the storehouse so that there would be food in Your house...." If you are not a tither or are not following the conditions of the Scripture, then you may want to start tithing before you apply the Word. Or, you may want to tell God that your intention is to start tithing; then you can begin to obey the scriptural condition immediately.

- **Exclude "narrative phrases" from your prayer.**

In Malachi 3:10-12, *"says the Lord of hosts"* is what I refer to as a narrative phrase. These phrases help narrate the story. Since you are talking to the Lord of hosts, you don't have to say, "says the Lord of hosts."

- **Feel free to insert what I call "declarative terms" as you are praying the Word.**

There are four commonly used declarative terms:

I decree.

I declare.

I confess.

I expect.

Don't those words carry a feeling of authority and power? Using them will help you actualize the authority that God has given you to speak His Word.

Here are some examples of how to use declarative terms in your prayers: "Father, I confess that I will bring all of my tithes into Your storehouse." "Father I declare that all the nations will call me blessed, and I will be a delightful land." "Father, I decree and declare that mercy and truth will not forsake me." "Father, I expect the devourer to be rebuked for my sake so that the fruit of my ground is not destroyed."

Section 3: Praying for Your Needs

Give us this day our daily bread.

This is probably the most familiar section to the believer, the prayer to ask God's provision for our wants and needs. In Philippians 4:6-7, Paul presents a powerful approach to praying for our personal needs:

Be anxious for nothing, but in everything by prayer and supplication, with thanksgiving, let your requests be known to God; and the peace of God, which surpasses all understanding, will guard your hearts and minds through Christ Jesus.

It is not difficult for us to "ask"; asking is what we do all of the time. Immediately, after giving God a brief praise, the believer makes a request. "Father, help us," or "Father, show us," or "Father, make us," or "Father, do it for us."

Evidently, making requests is appropriate because it is included in The Model Prayer. However, our requests are not the first order of business; they should be made later in our conversations with and for God.

That is why our personal requests are part of Section 3. Within this section about "our daily bread," two discussions arise: the believer's right to make requests and the believer's call to trust God for all he needs.

The Believer's Right to Ask

God's Word gives us the right to petition Him concerning our life's business. In our passage from Philippians, we are even encouraged to do so with a promise of peace. Isn't it comforting to know that the Father wants us to be assured that it is okay to ask Him for things we need?

Some of us don't ask because we don't think we deserve what we are asking for. Some of us don't ask because we don't want to bother God with our "little" problems or desires. Others of us don't ask because we don't think there is a remote possibility that what we want can be given.

God doesn't limit us, but often we do. As His children, we can ask Him for anything, great or small, be it material, spiritual, emotional, financial, or anything else, as long as our requests align with His Word.

Not only are we empowered to ask, we can be hopeful that our requests will be granted. How do we put ourselves in a position to receive our requests? By praying God's Word, of course! Remember, when He hears His Word, He hears us.

Think about that for a moment. We have the attention of the Lord God Almighty, the King of kings, waiting on us to ask Him what we want. Shouldn't we make sure we give Him the honor He deserves by being properly prepared before we ask?

If you wanted to achieve a top grade on a test, wouldn't you study until you felt confident you could correctly answer the questions? If you were going to court and wanted the judge to rule in your favor, wouldn't you build your case beforehand to gain a better chance for your desired verdict?

The Lord deserves no less preparation from us. In addition to identifying the appropriate Scriptures to pray, there are two things we should do to be ready to pray our requests:

1. Be specific. The Lord knows all things, but He wants His children to be specific. Don't we, as parents, want the same thing from our children?

In our home, our children know that fruit is a preferred snack and sweets are a special treat. When my oldest son was six, he walked into the kitchen and began to stare at me with a big Texas grin on his face. I had seen that stare and smile before, and I knew that he wanted something. After a long minute, he asked, "Mommy may I have…?" and then averted his eyes in the direction of the sweets.

I said, "Son what is it that you want?"

He simply replied, "Mommy, you know."

"No," I stated, "I do not know. What is it that you want?"

Again, he averted his eyes in the direction of the sweets and said, "You know."

I bent down to look him in the eye and said, "Son I do not know what you want, and if you do not tell me what it is, you will not get it."

Once again, with a smile that would light up the darkest room, he looked back into my eyes and said, "Mommy, you know."

By this time, I had become tired of this little game, and I told him, "Son, you will never receive what you want unless you tell me exactly what it is. I cannot read your mind, and I will not guess what you want."

With a hopeful sigh, he finally asked for the sweets. Since he hadn't had any that day, I gave them to him, and he walked away happy.

Like my son, you must tell God exactly what it is you want. Although He knows what it is, He expects you to be specific when you ask.

If you want a raise, determine the amount and ask God for it. Maybe you want a new home. How much are you willing to pay for your new home? Ask for that amount.

Some of us feel uncomfortable about asking for material items or anything that might benefit us personally. But remember, Philippians

4:6 says, *"Be anxious for nothing, but in everything by prayer and suppli-cation, with thanksgiving, let your requests be made known to God...."* His Word also tells us that He knows the thoughts we are thinking anyway, so we might as well be honest with Him and speak up. Make the request. I can't promise you He will say "Yes," but according to His will, you will be answered. In addition to material requests, lift up spiritual requests. Ask God for more wisdom, keener discernment, increased anointing, or abundant joy. These requests are always granted because they promote God's Kingdom and bring Him glory.

Being specific—whether you are praying for healing, peace of mind, spiritual maturity, a new car, your child's educational success, your cousin's marriage, improved finances, or the abatement of world hunger—enables the Holy Spirit to start speaking to you about your requests. He will give you the ideas necessary to address them. He may put a friendly children's tutor or marriage counselor next to you in the grocery checkout line. He may draw your attention to a television docu-mentary about ways to achieve emotional health or a newspaper article announcing a new treatment for your illness. An idea could pop into your mind about how to raise money for your household or how to start a nonprofit to grow and distribute food efficiently. Or, you might be put in the right place at the right time to save the life of a Ferrari salesman.

2. Think it through. If you are unsure about your request, spend some time thinking about what you want from the Lord. For example, if you are asking Him for a home for your family, allow Him to inform your desires. His guidance will keep you from buying a home that would break your budget or cause financial ruin.

The Believer's Call to Trust God

One would think that beliefs about asking God to "give us our daily bread" would be crystal clear. Yet, William Barclay states that The Model Prayer can be interpreted several ways.[13] Augustine, a fifth cen-tury priest, saw this portion of the prayer as the "sacrament of Christ's

Body which we receive daily." [14] It has been understood to mean to give us our "spiritual food, namely, the divine precepts which we are to think over and to put into practice each day." [15] Another interpretation understood this prayer to be referring to Christ. "Our daily bread is nothing less than Christ, the Bread of Life." [16]

I believe that Barclay captures the meaning by saying:

We need not for a moment deny that all these meanings may be in this petition. But we believe that the meaning of this petition is much simpler than any of these things. We believe that it is just what it says, that it is a petition for daily bread, a petition that God should give to us the simple, ordinary things which we daily need to keep body and soul together. It is in fact one of the most precious things in life that we can take the simple, ordinary things to God, that God is not only of the great world-shaking, epoch-making events, but that he is also the God who cares that his humblest child may have daily bread to eat. [17]

When we ask God to *"give us this day our daily bread,"* we are telling Him that we trust Him to provide our portion for the day. Furthermore, we know with certain confidence that our daily bread exists, and we believe that God, in His infinite wisdom, will move Heaven and earth to make sure that we have what we need.

The psalmist writes in Psalm 37:25, *"I have been young, and now am old; yet I have not seen the righteous forsaken, nor His descendants begging bread."* What a declaration of God's faithfulness! We do not have to beg for bread because God provides the bread.

In Exodus 16, God's faithfulness and provision are demonstrated through the Israelites' wilderness experience. The children of Israel complained about the lack of food and began to remember the full bellies they had as slaves in Egypt.

God, hearing their whining and complaining, spoke to Moses and promised to send manna (bread) and quail (meat) to satisfy their hunger. God ended His discussion with Moses by saying that they *"shall know that I am the Lord your God"* (verse 12).

The next morning, the ground was covered with manna and the quail flew in that evening. Moses instructed the people to take only what they needed for the day; anymore would be too much. God provided for the Israelites in this way for the entire 40 years they were in the wilderness.

God continues to provide our daily bread if we will allow Him. Can you trust God to give you what you need for the day? You may say, "My bills are overdue"…"My child's tuition is due"…"I want to invest in prime real estate, but I do not have enough money"…"I need peace of mind"…"I am sick, and I need help." Whatever the need, God can provide it, and He provides daily.

Will you trust Him to produce what you need today? Many times, believers try to make things happen and draw rigid boundary lines concerning their faith. If they do not have what they need in the timeframe *they want it,* they take matters into their own hands and interrupt God's plans and timing. Rabbi Eleazar Hagadol is known for saying, "Everyone who has food in his basket today and says, 'What will I eat tomorrow?'— behold, he is among those of little faith."[18]

Allow God's Word to strengthen your confidence in His faithfulness:

Trust in the Lord with all your heart, and lean not on your own understanding; in all your ways acknowledge Him and He shall direct your paths.[19]

God is our Provider. Depend upon God to provide for you today, and don't worry about tomorrow. He is concerned about us each day of our lives.

Give us this day our daily bread—then it is a gift, that daily bread. It comes to us from God in His great bounty and in His compassion for His hungry children.[20]

Ultimately, we want to end up saying *"Give us this day our daily bread"* and trust the Lord to provide for the day.

I find that exercising our faith to this extent takes time and practice. First, most believers are used to always asking God for their wants and needs. Second, it takes practice to yield your entire day to the governance of God without advising Him on what needs to happen. Therefore, I believe that taking one step of faith at a time will eventually get you to God's intended destination.

How to Make Your Request

Suppose you are struggling with your finances and you want to ask the Lord to bring increase in that area of your life. The following steps will strengthen your request for the greatest results:

1. Make a list. List at least 5-7 specific requests concerning your finances. There is nothing special about the number, but listing your requests will help you to specify what it is you really want from God. For example, you might ask to:

Receive a pay raise or promotion

Pay delinquent property taxes

Pay off a credit card debt

Place a down payment on a new house

2. Choose one request from your list.

3. Get specific. Think the request through. For example, your request may be to receive a pay raise at your job. How much increase do you want? This is the first question that needs to be answered. Is it all right to be this specific? Yes! You need to know how much more income you really want to receive. At first blush, you might say, "I want a million dollars." But, do you really want a million dollar increase if your annual income is nowhere near that amount? What qualifies you to receive such a pay raise? Are you willing to meet the additional responsibilities the pay raise would entail? What will you do with the extra income? Are you a good steward of your present income? Do you pay your tithes? Are you willing to pay the additional required taxes? Will your love for God change if He blesses you with a raise? These are just a few of the questions that should be answered so that you are better prepared to receive what God has planned for you.

4. Make your request. Once you have thought through your request and have answered any outstanding questions about it, you can make your request without hesitation or reservation.

CHAPTER 7

PRAY "THE MODEL PRAYER"—PART III

When you pray, know before Whom you stand.
—The Talmud

You are already becoming an experienced pray-er of scriptural prayers based on the pattern Jesus provided—and you are about to gain even more experience through the final three sections of The Model Prayer.

Section 4: Praying for Forgiveness

And forgive us our debts, as we forgive our debtors.

We have given the Lord praise, attended to His business, and petitioned Him for our needs. Now it is time to come clean before Him.

I find it interesting that we are halfway through the prayer and have had quite a bit of conversation with the Lord before we have had to address forgiveness. A good number of us have been taught that we must ask for forgiveness at the beginning of our prayer or God won't listen to the rest of our prayer. The Model Prayer, however, dispels that teaching as a myth and reveals a God who loves us more than He is bothered by our errors. His first priority is not our sin. His first priority is His relationship with us, His creation.

The Lord really is "in our corner." Not only does He love us, but He also likes us, and He enjoys talking and working with us. The Model Prayer demonstrates His sincere interest in us as His children. We can talk and commune with God, potentially for hours, as we praise Him, declare His Word, and make our requests known to Him before we ever have to repent.

Yet, like a loving parent, God will not allow us to leave our prayerful conversations without acknowledging our sins and seeking His forgiveness. Through Jesus, our sins have been forgiven; therefore, when we need His forgiveness, we simply have to ask for it with a sincere heart.

That is why Jesus left a model of prayer that put praying for forgiveness further down in the conversation. Our "mess" is not the most important topic of the day. It is within this environment of unconditional love that we can feel safe in acknowledging our sins and leaving them with Him.

But what is sin? What exactly are we asking God to forgive? *Sin* is defined as "missing the mark."[1] The "mark" consists of the instructions and requirements put forth by God through the Bible—including His instruction regarding characteristics such as marital fidelity, sexual purity, truthfulness, honesty, and respect for the lives and belongings of others.

By contrast to the "mark" God established in His Word, adultery, fornication, lying, cheating, murder, and stealing are commonly known acts of sin. When we commit them, we are missing the mark.

These actions go against God's divine plans for our lives, though in today's culture, they are often celebrated. It seems the more one lies, cheats, or commits adultery the more acclaim is given.

One of the most famous tourist destinations in the world is nicknamed "Sin City." But, no matter how attractive sin appears to be, it will eventually lead to heartache, disappointment, and worse. Romans 6:23 states that *"...the wages of sin is death...."*

Yet, there is more to missing the "mark" than just committing acts of sin. In my opinion, the greatest way to miss the mark is by not trusting and believing in God. When we do not trust Him completely and believe in Him wholeheartedly, we take life into our own hands. Ultimately, we become slaves to our passions and desires, which usually leads us to do and say things that do not represent Christ in us.

It is impossible for us to hit the "mark" when we are in the driver's seat of life. God knew this; He sent His Son to make the "mark" reachable and sent the Holy Spirit to help us overcome our fleshly urges. If you are battling with fleshly urges, ask the Holy Spirit to help you to overcome them. Using His power, you can conquer the source of the urges and make the right choices. The Holy Spirit is always available to empower you to live a godly life, and He is delighted when you are victorious. Psalm 89:17 says that God is our glorious strength, and it pleases Him to make us strong. Trying to defeat these urges in your own strength will leave you frustrated and feeling hopeless. Trust the Holy Spirit and let Him operate in your life.

In the end, hitting the "mark" depends on us. We must choose who the driver controlling our lives will be. Jesus said, *"I have come that they may have life, and that they may have it more abundantly."*[2] That promise includes you. Today, choose to obtain the "mark" through the help of the Holy Spirit. It is possible; you simply have to make a choice.

In this section of The Model Prayer, God wants us to accomplish two things: He wants us to ask Him for forgiveness, and He wants us to forgive other people.

1. Ask Him for forgiveness. We are given the opportunity to stand up before God and accept responsibility for our actions. As humans, it is seldom easy to admit our wrongs, particularly out loud. We want to sweep our issues under the rug or drive them so deep down in our consciousness that they lose their impact on the conscience. Or we try to minimize our wrongs by comparing them to the "greater" sins of others.

These tactics might work for a while, but we eventually realize that we cannot hide from God. He already knows everything we've done. He knows when we did it and to whom we did it. Yet He still waits patiently and lovingly for us to come with repentant hearts and genuine regret for our sins and tell Him. Not only will He hear us, He will take from us our guilt, remorse, self-hatred and any other negative emotions associated with our sins, leaving us free to go and sin no more.

As is true with our thanks and our requests to the Lord, we need to be specific in praying for forgiveness. "Lord, forgive me for lying to my boss about being sick because I wanted to take the day off." "Lord, I ask Your forgiveness for losing my temper with my mother because she treats me like I am still ten years old." "Lord, please forgive me for putting my work first and not attending my son's baseball game today." "Lord, You told me to give that man $10 and I only gave him $1; please forgive me."

When praying about a specific topic, such as finances, we are to reflect upon any errors we have committed in that area. It is always good to sit down and make a list. That forces us to really think about the role we have played in creating any adverse situations. The list regarding finances might include:

I don't tithe, or I haven't been tithing on a regular basis.

I have been spending more than I earn.

I haven't been teaching my children good stewardship over the money I give them.

When we go to God for forgiveness in each of these areas, our prayers might be:

Lord, Your Word says to pay tithes, which I have not been doing. I know I am supposed to and feel it in my spirit when I pass the offering basket on, but I still can't make myself do it. I always think that I am going to need that money for something else. I need Your help. Help me with my unbelief. Help me to put my trust in You. Forgive me for trying to control my financial destiny. Forgive me for robbing You by taking the money that belongs to You and using it for other purposes.

* * *

Oh, God, I purchased that suit today knowing that I did not have the extra money to do it. Once again, I am spending more than I am bringing home. It feels good when I buy something, but I am always crying toward the end of the month, wondering how I am going to pay my bills. This has got to stop. I submit this compulsion to You. Help me to be a better steward of Your gifts. Forgive me for overspending. Forgive me for jeopardizing our household budget.

* * *

Father, forgive me for wanting to be liked by my children more than I want to honor Your gifts. I have allowed my children to take the money I give them and spend it any way they want to, without teaching them to value what comes from You. When they *ask for more, I give it to them, even though it adversely affects our family budget. I gave John and Mary $10 today and, as usual, they didn't even thank me for it. Help me, Father, to love my children in a way that affirms them, yet prepares them to live prosperous lives. Help me understand what love truly is.*

* * *

It is to our benefit to be real with the Lord, not in a whining or proud way, but in a manner that shows Him we are sincerely contrite and eager to do better.

Even when we can't seem to stir up feelings of regret (particularly in cases where we've reacted to a wrong that was done to us), we need to ask forgiveness—both for our ungodly reactions and for our lack of regret. The Lord will deal with our hearts, encouraging our repentance.

2. Forgive others. What if you are blameless? What if you are going along, minding your own business, and a blow comes out of left field? A daughter steals money out of your purse to buy drugs. A friend blabs something you told him in confidence. Your relative refuses to admit to abusing you as a child. Your spouse falls in love with someone else and asks for a divorce.

It is no secret that we humans have a great capacity to hurt one another. Whether the pain comes from the smallest of slights or the most horrendous of acts, we are instructed to forgive those who have inflicted it.

That can be a tough pill to swallow. The Word, however, promises us a payoff—we get to be forgiven *if* we forgive. *"For if you forgive men their trespasses, your heavenly Father will also forgive you,"* says Jesus in Matthew 6:14. In verse 15, He goes on to say, *"But if you do not forgive men their trespasses, neither will your Father forgive your trespasses."* God believes in community, and He wants us to stay in good relationships with each other.

Many of our blessings are held up because we are unwilling to forgive. We hold on to our anger as if it were a prize. If we are honest with ourselves, we will admit that anger makes us feel superior and justified. It is as if our anger inflicts pain upon the person who hurt us.

I am not saying that we shouldn't get angry. It is a natural human emotion that God designed for us to express ourselves. Ephesians 4:26-27 says: *"Be angry, and do not sin: do not let the sun go down on your wrath, nor give place to the devil."* God expects us to get angry, but also to calm down and get things straight with each other.

We can maintain healthy relationships simply by communicating. When conflicts arise, we can open the door to healing by saying things such as:

"I am sorry about what I said." "I judged you too harshly." "I do not approve of your act, but I can try to understand why you did what you did."

If the person you need to forgive has died, write that person a letter and get all the pain out. Hold it up to the Lord and say, "I release this to You, God. I forgive *(name)* in Jesus' name." Tear up the letter and trust the Lord to heal your inner wounds (and He will). Resolve within yourself to go on with the rest of your life and never look back.

If you are harboring unforgiveness, yet still have experienced God's blessings, you may think that the Lord has given you special favor to be unforgiving. God does not act contrary to His Word. It is simply that His mercy, grace, and love for you have caused Him to prompt others to pray blessings into your life. The Lord hopes that, in receiving these blessings, you will turn to Him and trust Him in this area and forgive others because you have been blessed.

The ability to forgive will come instantaneously for some of us. For others, it will be extremely difficult, if not seemingly impossible. There is help. The Holy Spirit gives us the strength to move toward forgiveness. When we do so, the Lord will heal our wounds.

That doesn't mean that the person who hurt you has to be your friend or even that you need to see him or her again. You are to act according to God's will. Allow Him to inform your responses in every case.

He might tell you to give that person another chance and another and still another. Jesus instructs us in forgiveness through Matthew 18:21-35 (NLT), even saying that we are to forgive our brothers' sins against us 490 times:

> *Then Peter came to Him and asked, "Lord, how often should I forgive someone who sins against me? Seven times?" "No, not seven times," Jesus replied, "but seventy times seven!"*

> *"Therefore, the Kingdom of Heaven can be compared to a king who decided to bring his accounts up to date with servants who had borrowed money from him. In the process, one of his debtors was brought in who owed him millions of dollars. He couldn't pay, so his master ordered that he be sold—along with his wife, his children, and everything he owned—to pay the debt.*

> *"But the man fell down before his master and begged him, 'Please, be patient with me, and I will pay it all.' Then his master was filled with pity for him, and he released him and forgave his debt.*

> *"But when the man left the king, he went to a fellow servant who owed him a few thousand dollars. He grabbed him by the throat and demanded instant payment.*

"His fellow servant fell down before him and begged for a little more time. 'Be patient with me, and I will pay it,' he pleaded. But his creditor wouldn't wait. He had the man arrested and put in prison until the debt could be paid in full.

"When some of the other servants saw this, they were very upset. They went to the king and told him everything that had happened. Then the king called in the man he had forgiven and said, 'You evil servant! I forgave you that tremendous debt because you pleaded with me. Shouldn't you have mercy on your fellow servant, just as I had mercy on you?' Then the angry king sent the man to prison to be tortured until he had paid his entire debt.

"That's what My heavenly Father will do to you if you refuse to forgive your brothers and sisters from your heart."

If you have unforgiveness toward someone, then ask the Holy Spirit to help you to let go and forgive. Don't be like the debtor who refused to forgive a small debt after he was released from a massive debt that he could not possibly repay.

Without Jesus, we could never pay the debt we owe to God. But thanks be to God; our debt has been released through the blood of Jesus Christ, and forgiveness is granted us, simply for the asking.

If you are suffering from a wound that seems too deep to heal, then allow yourself to seek help from a professional counselor (preferably a Christian counselor). If you are unable to find a Christian counselor, find the best counselor you can, and ask the Holy Spirit to work through that person for your benefit. To be honest, ask the Holy Spirit to work through anyone with whom you counsel. I believe that professional counseling can help to root out the issues and offenses that are buried deep within. It can be hard to help yourself when you are in the middle of a storm. Let Jesus help you through the aid of another.

The importance of forgiveness cannot be overestimated. During a parenting seminar that I attended, Ms. Leona Ellis, Director of Children's Ministry for Windsor Village United Methodist Church, stated, "Unforgiveness is like drinking cyanide and expecting someone else to die." Why should we forgive others? Because we need forgiveness from our heavenly Father.

Let us not forget that forgiveness extends to us as well. The Lord expects us to love our neighbors and ourselves. In Luke 10:27, He says: *"You shall love the Lord your God with all your heart, with all your soul, with all your strength, and with all your mind, and your neighbor as yourself."*

Perhaps learning to love ourselves is the first priority so that we are able to love our neighbors as God has commanded. Our prayer might be, "Father, I will love You with all my heart and with all my soul and with all my strength and with all my mind; and I will love my neighbor as myself."

My suggestion is that the prayer would end with these words: "…and I will love myself."

An Exercise in Forgiveness

Perhaps you have read this far and still cannot face the prospect of forgiving the person who harmed you. You can't get past how unfair it would be for you to have to let the person off the hook.

Think about this: while you are mired in the pain of unforgiveness, the person you need to forgive has probably gone on with his or her life. It is time for you to do the same.

I am believing God right now that He can heal that place in your heart that is closed off due to hurt and unforgiveness. Would you pray with me? (Please pray this prayer aloud):

Father, we honor You for the meritorious work You performed through Your Son, Jesus Christ. Because of Christ, we have been set free of sin and given eternal life. Thank You for loving us beyond comprehension. Your Word says that we must forgive. You said that if we don't forgive people, You won't forgive us and we will not be able to live in Your Kingdom successfully: we cannot experience Your joy and peace. We cannot have a fruitful relationship with you—and we desire to have that. So Father, I am asking that You would touch the hearts of my sister or brother about the people they need to forgive, in Jesus' name.

Names and faces should start to come to your mind and to your attention. In your heart, begin to say, "Today, I am determined to forgive _____." (It may be your mother, father, co-worker, friend, spouse, relative, business partner, etc.)

Now say, as if the person were sitting right in front of you, "_____, I forgive you." Pray and ask God whether He would have you to call that person and share how deeply they hurt you. Please realize that there are circumstances in which initiating this conversation would not be helpful. In fact, in some cases, it may be ill-advised. If you feel that you should approach someone, before you talk with the person, consult with your pastor, a trusted friend, a prayer partner, or a counselor about the next steps of forgiveness. Anytime you have a conversation of this kind, stay humble and speak with love. "Kind words are like honey—sweet to the soul and healthy for the body."[3] Ask the Holy Spirit to help you stay calm; ask Him to saturate your being with His peace and give you the right words to say. Let the Holy Spirit guide you.

Maybe that person who offended you was too hard on you. Maybe she physically abused you. Maybe he cheated on you. Maybe she called you terrible names. Tell the offender what you are feeling—again, being certain that the Holy Spirit is guiding you. Once you have told the person how you feel, finish by saying, "I forgive you. I let you go. I forgive you."

As you have read this section, chances are that old hurts are being stirred up and old wounds are being exposed. Right now, let me pray with you for the healing of these wounds. Please pray the following prayer aloud:

> *Heavenly Father, we honor you as the only living God. Our God, you are kind and tender-hearted. Thank you for your continued blessings. In Jesus' name, I speak to my soul and tell it to be whole. Peace, be still in my soul. Jesus Christ bore my sins in His body so that I, having died to sin, could live for righteousness. By His stripes I have been healed. Today, I confess that my soul is brand new and, by faith, that I am healed from old wounds and memories. I will walk by faith and trust in the Lord with all of my heart. I will not focus on who offended me or how I was offended. Holy Spirit, purge me of anger, resentment, or bitterness. Destroy their roots. Create a clean heart and new spirit within me. Lord, forgive me for not giving you my offenses. In the future, I will forgive others and let you take care of my hurt feelings. Lord, forgive anyone reading this book who is holding on to offenses and help them to forgive others. Amen.*

If you need to ask the Lord to forgive you, do that now. Ask Him to forgive you for not being quick to forgive; for holding grudges; for responding in a cold, unfeeling manner; for saying hurtful words in order to be hurtful. Every person has his or her own individual experience. Talk to the Lord about your personal encounters.

Meanwhile, I invite you to pray this prayer aloud for restoration in your relationships and for any strongholds erected by unforgiveness to be dismantled:

Lord, I ask You to cleanse me from all unrighteousness and to forgive me of all of my sins. Thank You, Lord God. Now, Father, I am expecting the ruins of past relationships to be rebuilt and restored. I am expecting You, God, to close chapters and open new chapters in my life. I am expecting good results because of what You are doing in my life as I read this book. Help me to overcome any temptations to hold onto the past. Destroy the strongholds and defense mechanisms that have been constructed as a result of unforgiveness. Father, You can do anything; there is nothing too difficult for You. I pray in Jesus' name. Amen.

Now expect God to heal your heart and soul and to give you the courage to forgive.

Section 5: Praying for Protection

Do not lead us into temptation, but deliver us from the evil one.

Jesus knew there were two major forces His disciples would have to guard against—the power of their flesh and the power of demonic activity.

In Section 5 of The Model Prayer, Jesus instructed them, and now us, to protect ourselves by praying two statements: *"Do not lead us into temptation,"* and *"Deliver us from the evil one."*

Now, more than ever, we need the protection these statements offer. In today's world, there are myriad distractions. Daily, we are being seduced to commit acts that are self-destructive and ungodly.

Through this petition, we see that these distractions come from our own fleshly desires and through demonic activity. Prayer is necessary for overcoming the challenges brought on by these two forces. Be assured that, when you lift up this section of the prayer to God, help will always be provided.

Do not lead us into temptation. It could be thought that asking God not to lead us into temptation suggests that there is the possibility that He would lead us into temptation.

According to William Barclay, there are many translations of the phrase "lead us not into temptation" (as the King James Version verbiage states) with the emphasis being placed on the words lead and temptation.[4] Barclay goes on to say that some scholars translate the word "lead" to mean "to bring" as in "bring us not into temptation" or "do not subject" as in "do not subject us to temptation." "Lead" has been translated to mean "let us not" as in "let us not yield to temptation."[5] Says Barkley:

> When we come to think of it, this on the face of it is an extraordinary prayer, for in what sense can we ever believe that God would lead us into temptation? How could God ever be responsible for the attempt to seduce man into sin?[6]

I do not believe that God seduces people to sin. James 1:13-15 says, *"Let no one say when he is tempted, 'I am tempted by God'...."* The Bible also tells us that God makes a way for us to escape sin.[7]

God is never tempted to do wrong, and He never tempts anyone else to do wrong. Temptation comes from our desires, which entice us and drag us away. These desires give birth to sinful actions. And when sin is allowed to grow, it gives birth to death.

In my opinion, "let us not yield to temptation" would appear to better convey the meaning of *"do not lead us into temptation."* When you pray these words, you are asking God to help you to resist any temptation life might offer.

The word *temptation* is an image-rich word that can be applied to a multitude of situations. However, in this Scripture, the word *temptation* is not about having a carrot dangled in front of us, luring us to do something we should not do. It is about facing the inevitable trials and tests that come (whether through fleshly or demonic action), and trusting God to help us overcome them.

Temptation comes from the Greek word *peirasmos*,[8] which refers to trying or proving something. Life is filled with temptation, and it cannot be avoided. Throughout the Scriptures, God allowed people to be tested to see if their love for Him was genuine. In Deuteronomy 13:3, Moses states that God is *"testing you to know whether you love the Lord your God with all your heart and with all your soul."*

You may feel like you do not need to be tested by life in order to prove your love and faith for God, but in actuality, our flesh or human nature does not automatically gravitate toward God. Paul, in Galatians 5:17, states that our flesh wars against the nature of God and makes it difficult for us to carry out even our best intentions. Testing helps to rein in our human nature and submit it to God's leadership.

God tested Abraham's faith and loyalty by ostensibly requiring Isaac's life.[9] Abraham had waited 25 years for the son promised to him by God. During Abraham's day, people believed that they lived everlastingly through their offspring. That was their concept of everlasting life.

Why would God give this long-awaited gift only to ask Abraham to give it back? I believe God wanted to see whether Abraham loved Him more than he loved the gift. I also believe God wanted Abraham to know that he (Abraham) loved God more than he loved Isaac. What a demonstration of faith!

Abraham was chosen by God to be the father of God's chosen people. The promise of God's covenant would be fulfilled through Abraham's loins—his generations. The question was: would Abraham fulfill his commitment to God and follow Him with an unshakeable faith?

This test would produce the answer. Abraham and Isaac ascended the mountain on a path of uncertainty and hope—uncertainty about the purpose of the test, but hope in the promise of God.

I can imagine that Abraham's flesh did not want to obey God. Isaac was his son, his long-anticipated promise, and his future. I am sure that it was not easy for him to climb that mountain with Isaac and carry the knife that would soon end his son's destiny.

Abraham was unsure of the outcome, but he knew that he had to obey God. Isaac, unknowingly carrying the wood for his own sacrifice, asked, *"My father!... Where is the lamb for a burnt offering?"*[10]

I believe that Abraham passed the test when he answered, *"My son, God will provide for Himself the lamb for a burnt offering."*[11] Abraham remembered what God had promised him about his son, and he trusted God for the fulfillment of His promise.

When we pray, *"Do not lead us into temptation,"* we are not asking to escape temptation, but to overcome it. We are asking God to help us not to yield or fail the test, but to be with us and protect us during the test with the assurance that He will help us to be victorious.

The victory won by faith in God is not only seen in the outcome of the battle—it is also seen in the change within. There is an old saying that "trials come to make us strong." James writes in James 1:2-4:

> *Dear brothers and sisters, when troubles come your way, consider it an opportunity for great joy. For you know that when your faith is tested, your endurance has a chance to grow. So let it grow, for when your endurance is fully developed, you will be perfect and complete, needing nothing* (NLT).

Given the option, few of us would raise our hands and volunteer to undergo difficulties. Challenges are simply a part of life. They are natural by-products of living. When they come, we can raise our voices and ask the Lord to help us, expecting that He will. When the difficulties pass, we realize that we have been molded and shaped in a way that strengthens character and increases integrity.

The Lord leads us through and, in turn, we are more loyal to Him. We are stronger in our faith and better equipped to be used by Him. When the next trial or test comes, we are not tempted to turn away from Him; instead, we turn toward Him for protection.

When we pray, *"Do not lead us into temptation,"* God's Word watches over us to prevent harm. We can ask Him for protection over us, our families, or our neighbors. He will protect us from anything seen or unseen.

But deliver us from the evil one. *"But deliver us from the evil one"* defends us against any plans the devil has devised against us. The devil is always contriving ways to distract and ensnare us. After all, Peter reminded us that the devil *"walks about like a roaring lion, seeking whom he may devour."*[12]

The devil's goal is to break the covenant relationship between God and humanity. He has no allegiance to God, and he is determined to destroy all that God has intended for humanity. It is our responsibility to be knowledgeable of his devices and to denounce them.

The fight against the devil has been called spiritual warfare. It is the battle that the devil attempts to wage with us through our thoughts and actions. The devil's first level of attack is usually through the mind, as Second Corinthians 10:4-5 demonstrates:

For the weapons of our warfare are not carnal but mighty in God for pulling down strongholds, casting down arguments and every

high thing that exalts itself against the knowledge of God, bring-
ing every thought into captivity to the obedience of Christ...

The devil says things to us that are subtle and often simple. He says just enough to get us to wonder whether God's way is right. Eve encountered the craftiness of the devil. He posed a seemingly simple question to her, *"Did God really say...?"³* This was enough to cause Adam and Eve to question the infallibility of God's words.

Before a sinful action is ever committed, a sinful thought is introduced. When we pray *"deliver us from the evil one,"* we are asking the Holy Spirit to combat any wicked thoughts introduced by the devil and to help us to not yield to those thoughts.

How do we reduce the infiltration of the devil's thoughts? We reduce them through the washing of God's Word. Reading and declaring God's Word every day will overthrow any demonic interference. Isaiah 26:3 assures us that we will have *"perfect peace"* when our minds are fixed on God.

We must be careful not to put ourselves in situations where we can be attacked by the devil. If we pray for God's protection, but make decisions to do things we know we should not do, we make ourselves targets for the enemy.

Without the power of the Holy Spirit, we are no match for the devil. But, we are not without power; we are full of God's spirit and subsequently His power, and through His assistance, we will triumph over any onslaughts.

The devil is a defeated foe. When Jesus completed His work on earth and returned to our heavenly Father through the resurrection and ascension, He destroyed the devil's power over humanity. We are free from the stranglehold of sin and death, and we are more than conquerors. As you pray Section 5 of The Model Prayer, pray with the confidence and assurance of knowing that Jesus has all power to help you overcome the devil. And Jesus is willing to do it!

To pray *"Do not lead us into temptation, but deliver us from the evil one"* is to admit the reality of the dangerous situations life presents, the inability of humankind to handle these situations, and the urgent need for God's protective power.

Section 6: Kingdom Praise and Worship

> *For Yours is the kingdom and the power and the glory forever. Amen.*

If praise and worship is the appropriate way to approach the Lord, it is an equally appropriate way to end our prayer time.

The Model Prayer presents a pattern that begins with praise and ends with praise. It reminds us to honor and revere God at the beginning and the end of our prayerful conversations with Him.

However, there is a difference between Sections 1 and 6. When we enter the presence of the Lord, we are to address Him as our Father and converse with Him as a child would converse with his parents— through conversation that is filled with trust and confidence, knowing that God has committed Himself to love and nurture us.

The praise and worship in this final section is offered from a different perspective; it reflects our relationship as citizens of the Kingdom of God. *"For Yours is the kingdom and the power and the glory"* speaks of the sovereignty and awesomeness of God. Yes, He is our Father, but we must never forget that He is God of the universe.

We come to the throne saying "Daddy." We leave saying, "King." Ephesians 2:19 states that *"Now, therefore, you are no longer strangers and foreigners, but fellow citizens with the saints and members of the household of God."* As such, we are to pay homage to the King of the Kingdom, the Almighty God, the Lord of Heaven's Armies.

For example, when the children of the president of the United States are at home with him, he is "Dad" to them. But when he is at work, his official capacity as president supersedes his role as their dad. His children must respect his office and abide by the same laws as any other citizen relating to him as their president. If the president's children were to come against him in any illegal way, they would be subject to the same consequences as all other citizens of the United States.

The prayer uttered in this final section of The Model Prayer is exclusively for God. Every word that is spoken must venerate His Kingship. This section does not contain the words, *I, me,* or *my.* There are no statements such as "I think You are wonderful"; "You are so good to me"; or "My soul delights in You."

This praise is not dependent upon what we think or how we feel about God. There is only adoration and praise for Him. Human beings are left out of this part of The Model Prayer. God is the center and the sole beneficiary of our praise.

Once again, we can use the Scriptures to honor the Lord. Revelation 4:11 and 5:12 provide amazing expressions of praise that fit perfectly into the final portion of The Model Prayer:

> *You are worthy, O Lord, to receive glory and honor and power; for You created all things, and by Your will they exist and were created.*

> *Worthy is the Lamb who was slain to receive power and riches and wisdom, and strength and honor and glory and blessing!*

Let these perfect words become your personal praise to the King of kings and the Lord of lords–and use the exercises below to personalize a new scriptural prayer and express your praise.

Exercise 1: Prayer of Praise and Adoration (from Psalm 89:5-8 NLT)

Scripture Passage

All heaven will praise your great wonders, Lord; myriads of angels will praise You for Your faithfulness. For who in all of heaven can compare with the Lord? What mightiest angel is anything like the Lord? The highest angelic powers stand in awe of God. He is far more awesome than all who surround His throne. O Lord God of Heaven's Armies! Where is there anyone as mighty as you, O Lord? You are entirely faithful.

Scriptural Prayer

All heaven will praise your great wonders, Lord; myriads of angels will praise You for Your faithfulness. For who in all of heaven can compare with _____, Lord? What mightiest angel is anything like _____? The highest angelic powers stand in awe of _____. _____ are far more awesome than all who surround _____ throne. O Lord God of Heaven's Armies! Where is there any as mighty as _____, O Lord? _____ are entirely faithful.

(See Appendix E for the completed version of this prayer.)

Exercise 2: Prayer of Praise and Adoration (from Jeremiah 10:12-16 NLT)

Scripture Passage

But God made the earth by His power, and He preserves it by His wisdom. With His own understanding He stretched out the heavens. When He speaks in the thunder, the heavens roar with rain. He causes the clouds to rise over the earth. He sends the lightning with the rain and releases the wind from His storehouses. The whole human race is foolish and has no knowledge! The craftsmen are disgraced by the idols they make, for their carefully shaped works are a fraud. These idols have no breath or power. Idols are worthless; they are ridiculous lies! On the day of reckoning they will all be destroyed. But the God of Israel is no idol! He is the Creator of everything that exists, including Israel, His own special possession. The Lord of Heaven's Armies is His name!

Scriptural Prayer

God, you made the earth by _____ power, and _____ preserve it by _____ wisdom. With _____ own understanding _____ stretched out the heavens. When _____ speak in the thunder, the heavens roar with rain. _____ cause the clouds to rise over the earth. _____ send the lightning with the rain and release the wind from _____ storehouses. The whole human race is foolish and has no knowledge! The craftsmen are disgraced by the idols they make, for their carefully shaped works are a fraud. These idols have no breath or power. Idols are worthless; they are ridiculous lies! On the day of reckoning they will all be destroyed. But,_____, God of Israel, are no idol! _____ are the Creator of everything that exists, including Israel,_____ own special possession. The Lord of Heaven's Armies is _____ name!

(See Appendix E for the completed version of this prayer.)

CHAPTER 8

WALK THE TALK

The best of all teachers, experience.
—Pliny the Younger

We have discussed each section of The Model Prayer and have developed several examples of personalized, scriptural prayers to use while praying through the sections.

Next, we'll expand our horizons by applying what we have learned to real-life prayer opportunities that reach beyond our own lives and homes to touch our communities, our political system, and our nation. It's what I call "walking the talk."

But first, let's pull together all of the information we have covered so far and develop a quick section-by-section checklist for productive prayer. The following pointers will help you to stay on track, whatever the prayer focus:

Section 1: Intimate Praise and Worship

1. Acknowledge God as Father.

2. Communicate with God like a child communicates with his parents.

3. Offer thanksgiving that is specific to your topic.

4. Offer adoration and reverence, and use Scripture to extol Him.

5. Be intentional and passionate.

Section 2: Praying God's Will

1. Take time to identify the appropriate Scriptures for your prayer focus. Do not arbitrarily pray Scriptures.

2. Understand the meaning of the Scripture, and always pray Scripture in context.

3. Pray Scriptures confidently and in faith. *Remember that you are sending His word into the supernatural to retrieve His plans and bring them into earthly reality.*

4. Declare, Decree, Confess, Expect.

Section 3: Praying for Your Needs

1. Lift up your requests, and keep them specific to your prayer focus.

2. In addition to material requests, lift up spiritual requests.

Section 4: Praying for Forgiveness

1. Ask! Ask! Ask! for forgiveness that is specific to your prayer focus. Be real with God. Search within yourself and remain transparent before God.

2. Be specific about who you want to forgive. Ask the Holy Spirit to help you to release offenses and to be patient with people.

3. Be quick to forgive.

Section 5: Praying for Protection

1. Pray *"Lead us not into temptation, but deliver us from the evil one."*

2. I teach my students to stick with this statement since many of them do not have experience in spiritual warfare. Because our words are so powerful, we must use caution when speaking to the devil or rebuking demonic forces. This simple statement is God's Word, and it is more than adequate to provide the protection we need.

Section 6: Kingdom Praise and Worship

1. Use Scripture to declare the sovereignty and awesomeness of God.

2. Honor God like a citizen of a kingdom honoring a king.

3. Take the "I's" out of this paragraph and focus entirely on God. Remember that this section is not about us—it belongs solely to Him.

4. Leave your prayer session with reverence, passion, expectation, and mountain-moving faith.

Power-Packed Prayer!

In Chapter 1, "Productive Prayer," I mentioned the "prayer productivity rate." This is the rate at which God's plans in Heaven are produced on earth. By praying The Model Prayer, we are able to increase our spiritual effectiveness as God's partners to achieve His will and increase our prayer productivity rate.

That is the amazing thing about using this pattern set forth by Jesus: our prayers become increasingly effective because they are based, not on our power, perfection, or ability, but on His Word, which is 100 percent potent, accurate, and efficacious.

The Model Prayer keeps our prayers strategic, powerful, and on target. Remember, we are the "voice" of God. When we speak His Word, using His prayer strategy, our prayer vehicle carries His Word into the supernatural where its job description and all of its job functions work to retrieve God's plans and deliver them back to the earth. Once we see the results manifested, we can consider God's mission accomplished.

When Jesus told the disciples to pray The Model Prayer, I believe He intended for them—and us—to have a successful "prayer productivity rate."

The Model Prayer for Every Occasion

The Model Prayer can be applied to any situation or occasion simply by articulating each section as it regards to the prayer topic at hand.

The remainder of this chapter contains examples of prayers that have been written to pray about a variety of topics and events.

Remember that the key to praying powerful, productive prayers is to articulate them according to the order presented in The Model Prayer and to pray them aloud. To illustrate the pattern clearly, these examples have been broken down into the six sections we have studied. (Please note: when you distribute prayers like these for public use, you can forego the section subheadings; they are inserted here for instructional purposes only.) Make sure you pray the sections in the order they are represented in The Model Prayer. You will notice that the length of the prayers varies. As mentioned in the Introduction, the power of our prayers is not in how long we pray, but in what we say when we pray. When constructing your prayer, be sure that the content of your prayer is Scripture-based, factually relevant, and aligned with The Model Prayer.

Example 1: Prayer for U.S. Presidential Inauguration

Intimate Praise and Worship

O Lord, Our God, how excellent is Your Name in all the Earth! You are great and greatly to be praised! We conclude the 55th inaugural ceremony with an attitude of thanks. Thank You for protecting America's borders. After all, as the psalmist reminds us, unless the Lord guards the territory, our efforts will be in vain. Thank You for our military personnel. And, it is with unswerving thanksgiving that we pause to remember the persons who have made the ultimate sacrifice to help ensure America's safety. Thank You, O Lord, for surrounding our military personnel, their families, their friends, and our allies with Your favor and faithfulness.

Praying God's Will

Deploy Your hosts from Heaven so that Your will for America will be performed on earth as it is already perfected in Heaven. I confess that Your face will shine upon the United States of America, granting us social peace and economic prosperity, particularly, for the weary and the poor. I also confess that each American's latter days will be better than their former days. Let it be unto us according to Your Word!

Praying for Your Needs

Rally the Republicans, the Democrats, and the Independents around Your common good so that America will truly become one Nation under God, indivisible, with liberty, justice, and equal opportunity for all, including the least, the last, and the lost. Bless every elected official across America right now! I decree Your blessings to shower upon President George W. Bush. Bless him, his family, and his administration. I declare no weapon formed against him or them will prosper.

Praying for Forgiveness

Forgive us. Forgive us for becoming so ensnarled in petty, partisan politics that we miss Your glory and flunk our purpose.

Praying for Protection

Deliver us from the evil one, from evil itself, and from the mere appearance of evil. Give us clean hearts so we may have clean agendas, clean programs, and clean financial statements.

Kingdom Praise and Worship

And now unto You, Lord God Almighty, who always has been and always will be the One true power broker and King of kings, we glorify and honor You. Respecting persons of all beliefs, I humbly submit this prayer in the Name of Jesus Christ, amen.[1]

Example 2: Prayer for the Houston Livestock Show and Rodeo

Intimate Praise and Worship

Heavenly Father, we honor You as God, Almighty. You are great and greatly to be praised. There is none like You. Thank You for blessing our great city. Thank You for blessing the Houston Livestock Show and Rodeo. Thank You for blessing those in attendance tonight and their families.

Praying God's Will

Today, I declare that the 2006 Houston Livestock Show and Rodeo will be safe, productive, and prosperous like never before. I decree your blessings over the leaders, participants, staff, volunteers, and fans. I confess that the Houston Livestock Show and Rodeo will continue to be a beacon of hope for the youth of Texas.

Praying for Your Needs

Lord let Your favor, protection, and provision surround this entire event.

Praying for Forgiveness

Forgive us for pursuing strategies that don't reflect You and Your ways.

Praying for Protection

Help this great organization to resist any temptations that would not please You and Lord, destroy any works of evil.

Kingdom Praise and Worship

Holy and awesome God, respecting all persons of different faiths, I humbly submit this prayer to You in Jesus' Name, amen.

Example 3: Prayer for the Greater Houston Partnership

Intimate Praise and Worship

Father, before the people You created, I honor You. You are great and your name is great and mighty. Thank You for blessing our great city. Thank You for blessing this historic day. Today, I declare that the prosperity and productivity of the greater Houston economy will flourish like never before.

Praying God's Will

I confess that justice will run down as waters and righteousness as a mighty stream. I decree that the greater Houston area will become on earth what You have already established in Heaven.

Praying for Your Needs

Lord, bless the Greater Houston Partnership, chairman-elect Jodie Jiles and the food that we are about to receive.

Praying for Forgiveness

Forgive us for pursuing strategies that don't reflect You and Your ways.

Praying for Protection

Help the Partnership to resist any temptations that would not please You and destroy any works of evil.

Kingdom Praise and Worship

Holy and awesome God, respecting all persons who call on another name, I humbly submit this prayer to you in Jesus' Name, amen.

Example 4: A Prayer for the 2008 Economic Crisis in the United States of America

Intimate Praise and Worship

Heavenly Father, You are God, and Your Word is true. We exalt You, our God and King. We will praise Your Name forever and ever. Every day we will praise You. You are most worthy of praise. You are our source, and we place our trust in You. Holy and Righteous is Your Name. You are a great God and a great King above other gods. You are our God; we are Your people who You watch over. We are the flock under Your care. Thank You for blessing the United States of America throughout the years. Thank You, Father, for blessing the economic infrastructure of our nation. Thank You for surrounding our nation with Your favor, grace, and mercy during this time of economic crisis. Thank You for hearing the righteous, as we cry out to You on behalf of our nation. Thank You, Lord, for being our source, supply, and hope.

Praying God's Will

In Jesus' Name, we speak to the United States economy and all interrelated global economies and command "peace, be still" within and among all the economic systems. We stand in the authority given to us and speak to the economic infrastructure of our nation, and we command the United States credit markets to become calm and fluid. We also command all related financial intermediaries around the world to become calm and fluid. We command restoration to consumer and investor confidence. We command the banking industry to stabilize and the enterprise values of U.S. corporations to rebound supernaturally, now! As a result, we decree that DOW JONES, NASDAQ, and the major financial exchange networks around the world will rebound and thrive.

We command the housing industry to stabilize and home values to be restored to levels that will reflect God's biblical promises for this country. We rebuke the spirits of conspicuous consumption, fear, uncertainty, and inefficiency. In Jesus' Name, we boldly proclaim foreclosures to cease, job losses to reverse, and the stock market decline to bottom out. Peace, be still! As a Church Family, we confess that our Jehovah Jireh provides all of our economic needs according to His riches by Christ Jesus. Father, we thank You in advance for Your provision. We have never seen the righteous forsaken, nor God's children begging bread. During this economic downturn, we decree that our financial position in the world is strong and healthy. We speak normalcy and balanced prosperity back into our economic system.

Praying for Your Needs

Eternal Father, we ask that You would pour out Your wisdom, discernment, and divine understanding into Federal Reserve

Chairman Ben S. Bernanke, Treasury Secretary Henry Paulson, Barney Frank of the House Committee on Financial Services, and all local, state, and national economic and government leaders. Reveal creative ideas and effective methods to them that will decrease our national deficit while continuing to provide the necessary standards, services, and benefits to the American people. Holy Spirit, stir the hearts of the Body of Christ to stand and boldly proclaim Your Word concerning the current global and U.S. economic predicament. Please restore the confidence of the American people in You, as our source and supply, and remove any thoughts of fear or dismay. Holy Spirit, help government officials to put aside "politics" and to operate in the best interest of the American people.

Trouble the hearts of the House and Senate to approve legislation that will provide the proper oversight and regulations that will promote a stable and reliable economy. Almighty God, Lord of Heaven's Armies, protect our nation during this extremely vulnerable time in our history. Restore our international reputation and increase Your favor for our country. We admit that we don't deserve it, but You promise to hear our prayers and listen. Have mercy upon our nation. We need Your divine intervention. God, bless America!

Praying for Forgiveness

Lord, we repent on behalf of our nation for our many sins. Forgive us for ageism, sexism, racism, and nepotism. Forgive us for greed, arrogance, selfishness, imperialism, and oppression. Please forgive the financial intermediaries for charging more than they should have charged for packaging and securitizing the mortgages. Forgive CEO's for accepting extraordinary compensation while leaving Americans empty-handed. Forgive consumers who borrowed more money than they could pay back. Forgive our nation for financial irresponsibility and carelessness. Holy Spirit, show our leaders who they need to forgive; and help them to forgive.

Praying for Protection

As a nation, lead us not into temptation; but deliver us from the evil one.

Kingdom Praise and Worship

Lord, there is none like You. You are great, and Your Name is full of power. Who would not fear You, O King of the nations? That title belongs to You alone! Among all the wise people of the earth and in all the kingdoms of the world, there is no one like You. You are the King of glory. You are the Lord of Heaven's Armies. You are worthy, Lord our God, to receive glory, honor, and power. You created all things, and they exist because You created what You pleased.

The following prayers may be used to pray for specific topics and events in the years to come. Feel free to tailor the wording to the specific circumstances as needed.

Example 5: A Prayer of Adoration and Reverence for God and His Word

Intimate Praise and Worship

Father, today we proclaim Your Name, the Name of the Lord. You are glorious. You are our Rock, and Your deeds are perfect. Everything You do is just and fair. You are faithful, and You do no wrong. How just and upright You are! Your unfailing love toward those who fear You is as great as the height of the heavens above the earth. Let the whole world fear and stand in awe of You, Lord. You spoke and the world began; it appeared at Your command.

Lord, You are our inheritance and hope. Thank You, Father, for Your love and compassion. Thank You for keeping Your covenant with us throughout the ages. Thank You for making us Your people. What a joy it is to be one of Your children. Father, You are good, and Your faithful love endures forever.

Praying God's Will

Father, today, we reverence and honor You. You are our God, and we submit our loyalty and adoration to You. You are the Alpha and Omega, the beginning and the end. You existed before time and created everything that exists. We acknowledge that You are the only living God. There are no other gods. Father, You are compassionate and merciful, slow to get angry, and filled with unfailing love. You are good to everyone, and You shower compassion on all of Your creation. All of Your works will thank You, Lord, and we, Your followers, praise You. You are so awesome! We confess that we will keep Your commandments, walk in Your ways, and revere You. Father, we confess that Your instructions are perfect, reviving our souls. Your decrees are trustworthy, making wise the simple. Your commandments are right, bringing joy to our hearts. Your commands are clear, giving insight for living. Revering You is pure, lasting forever. Your laws are true and each one is fair. Father, Your Word is more desirable than gold, yes, even the finest gold. Your Word is sweeter than honey dripping from the honeycomb. Your Word warns us, and we expect great reward as we adhere to it. Father, You are great and greatly to be praised. We will bless You at all times and constantly speak of Your praises.

Praying for Your Needs

Father, please let Your ears be attentive to our prayer. Holy Spirit, teach us how to reverence and adore our Father in true holiness.

Please touch the hearts of those who do not reverence and adore You and help them to love You with all their hearts, souls, and strength. Holy Spirit, place in us a hunger and thirst for Your righteousness so that we will be filled.

Praying for Forgiveness

Father, forgive us for sins of pride, rebellion, disobedience, selfishness, hatred, and idolatry. Lord, forgive us for half-hearted worship. Forgive us for disrespecting Your Name and treating You irreverently. Forgive those of us who are parents for not teaching our children to revere and adore You. Lord, remind us of those we need to forgive; and help us to forgive.

Praying for Protection

Lead us not into temptation; but deliver us from the evil one.

Kingdom Praise and Worship

You are God alone; there is no other God, and there never has been, and there never will be. You are the Lord, and there is no other Savior. From eternity to eternity, You alone are God. All honor and glory belongs to You forever and ever! You are the eternal King, the unseen One who never dies; You alone are God. Yours is the Kingdom and the power and the glory forever. In Jesus' Name, Amen.

Example 6: Prayer for Blessing and Protection for School-children and Teachers

Intimate Praise and Worship

Father, we honor and bless Your holy name. We are Your people and the sheep of Your pasture. Thank You, Father, for our schools. Thank You for caring, professional teachers who will teach our children. We are thankful to You, and we bless Your name.

Praying God's Will

Father, we release blessings upon our schools. We declare that, like Jesus, our students will increase in wisdom and knowledge and that they will have favor with You, their classmates, their administrators, and their teachers. We confess that, during this school year, they will stay focused on their studies as if they were working for You. Lord, we confess that the teachers at our children's schools walk in love, joy, peace, patience, kindness, goodness, faithfulness, gentleness, and self-control.

Praying for Your Needs

Holy Spirit, help each student to remain focused and committed to his or her studies. Lord, please continue to protect each child, administrator, and teacher. Father, cause students, teachers, and parents to work with each other and to walk in peace. Encourage parents to be actively involved in their children's education.

Praying for Forgiveness

Father, forgive our teachers and students for all acts of sin. Forgive those teachers who are not patient, nurturing, or encouraging. Forgive our students for not being obedient to their teachers and parents. Forgive parents for not being involved with their children's education. Holy Spirit, remind all parties to forgive others, and help them to forgive.

Praying for Protection

Do not lead our students and teachers into temptation, but deliver them from the evil one.

Kingdom Praise and Worship

Lord, You are worthy to receive glory, honor, and power. You created all things, and by Your will they exist and were created. In Jesus' name, amen.

Example 7: Prayer for the U.S. Economy

Intimate Praise and Worship

Lord, You are King! You are robed in majesty and armed with strength. The world stands firm and cannot be shaken. Your throne, O Lord, has stood from time immemorial, and You Yourself are from the everlasting past. The floods have risen up; they roar like thunder and pound their waves. You are mightier than the raging of the sea and mightier than the breakers on the shore. Today we sing to You, Lord, and shout joyfully to You, the Rock of our salvation. We come with thanksgiving, singing songs of praise to You. Father, we thank You for being the Source of our supply. We thank you for meeting all of our needs from Your glorious riches, which have been given to us in Christ Jesus. Your name is a strong fortress that we, the godly, can run to and find safety.

Praying God's Will

Father, some nations boast of their chariots and horses; but we boast in the name of the Lord our God. As Your people, we stand in the authority You have given us and speak to the economic infrastructure of our nation. In Jesus' name, we command that:

- *U.S. credit markets become calm*

- *The U.S. buying and borrowing binge ceases*

- *Consumer and investor confidence be restored*

- *Economic growth continue and remain steady!*

We command justice to run down like water and righteousness like a mighty stream within our economy. We command the value of the U.S. dollar to increase in the international market. Father, the Word says death and life are in the power of the tongue; so as the people of God, we boldly call for new beginnings, increase, and abundance for our nation's economy now. We confess that the fiscal health of the United States is strong, stable, and vibrant.

Praying for Your Needs

Almighty Father, because this nation has stood under the banner of Your name, we thank You for hearing our declarations for the economy. Make a pathway in the wilderness and create rivers in the dry wastelands of our nation's economic system. Holy Spirit, reveal new strategies to the country's economic visionaries and strategists. Holy Spirit, help our government to make wise and godly decisions with our country's resources. Please deal with the hearts of each American family to live within their budget and to save and invest so that an inheritance can be passed on to future generations.

Praying for Forgiveness

Lord, we repent on behalf of our nation for our many sins. We repent for the sin of idolatry. Please forgive us for making money, sex, power, careers, entertainment, and personal interests our gods. Forgive us, as a nation, for not honoring the nuclear family structure, for disrespecting our elders, and for not investing in the lives of our children and youth. Forgive us for the corruption that exists within our judicial system and the greed that exists within our corporations. Forgive us for mismanaging the resources, wealth, and opportunities You have given to our nation. Forgive us for placing our trust and hope in the economy and not in You. Holy Spirit, show us those we need to forgive; and help us to forgive.

Praying for Protection

As a nation, do not lead us into temptation; but deliver us from the evil one.

Praise and Worship

Heavenly Father, we know through Your Word that all Your promises are "Yes" and "Amen" to your glory. We bless You, the Lord of Heaven's Armies, for Your home reaches up to the heavens, while its foundation is on the earth. You draw up water from the oceans and pour it down as rain on the land. The Lord is Your name! In the mighty name of Jesus, amen.[2]

Example 8: A Prayer for Our Family Members, Friends, Co-workers, and Enemies Who Have Not Accepted Jesus Christ as Their Lord and Savior

Intimate Praise and Worship

O Lord, our God, Your majestic name fills the earth. Your glory is higher than the heavens. Our souls bless You, and we will remember the good things You have done for us. You are the One who forgives all our sins, heals us from diseases, redeems us from death, and crowns us with love and tender mercies. You fill our lives with good things and renew our youth like the eagle's! We honor You as our Lord and Savior. Thank You for the gift of salvation through Your Son, Jesus Christ. We thank You for extending Your unfailing love toward us. Thank You, Father, for the tremendous harvest of souls in our city. You are great and deserving of all praise.

Praying God's Will

Father, it is Your will that prayers, intercessions, and thanksgiving be made for all men so that we can live peaceful and quiet lives marked by godliness and dignity. It is Your desire that all men be saved and understand the truth that You are the only God and there is only one Mediator who can reconcile humanity back to You—the man, Jesus Christ. Today, we acknowledge that Jesus Christ is the way, the truth, and the life. He is the only door by which people can be saved. Father, You are so rich in kindness and grace that You have purchased our freedom with the blood of Jesus Christ, Your Son, and have forgiven our sins. We declare, by faith, that [list names of nonbelievers] will confess with their mouths that Jesus is Lord and believe in their hearts that God raised Jesus from the dead, and we expect that they will be saved. Father, we decree that they will know the truth, and the truth will set them free. As for me, I confess my sins. I believe that You are faithful and just to forgive me of my sins and to cleanse me from all unrighteousness. I submit to You, my spirit, soul, and body.

Praying for Your Needs

Father, we ask You to clear the way so that Your Gospel may be preached in [name of your city]. As You know, the harvest is great. Please send laborers to proclaim Your Word of salvation to [list names of nonbelievers]. Holy Spirit, stir up their hearts and remove the darkness that keeps them from seeing and receiving You. As Your Word goes forth, Holy Spirit, please touch their hearts to receive Your gift of salvation. Holy Spirit, touch the hearts of believers who have strayed away from You, leading them to return to You and Your eternal love. Father, use me as an answer to this prayer and give me Your courage and boldness to witness Your love and salvation to nonbelievers.

Praying for Forgiveness

Father, forgive [list the names of nonbelievers] for not acknowledging You and receiving Your Son. Forgive them for all acts of sinfulness, including disobedience, hatred, rebellion, murder, idolatry, homosexuality, greed, racism, adultery, fornication, injustice, and violence. Please have mercy upon them and extend Your grace toward them. Forgive those believers who have strayed from You. Forgive us, the Body of Christ in [name of your city], for not sharing Jesus and the Gospel with more people. Forgive me for being timid and reserved about sharing the Gospel. Lord, remind all of us of those persons we need to forgive, and please help us to forgive.

Praying for Protection

Lead us not into temptation; but deliver us from the evil one.

Kingdom Praise and Worship

Lord, You alone have held the oceans in Your hand. You measured off the heavens with Your fingers. Only You know the weight of the earth and have weighed the mountains and hills on a scale. All the nations of the world are but a drop in the bucket to You; they are nothing more than dust on the scales. You pick up the whole earth as though it were a grain of sand. The Lord God Almighty is Your name. In Jesus' name, amen.

Example 9: A Prayer for Finances

Intimate Praise and Worship

Father, You are great, and You perform wonderful deeds. You alone are God. Lord, You are in Your Holy temple; You rule from Heaven. To You, O God, do we give thanks. Yes, to You do we give thanks. We thank You for Your eternal love and unmerited grace.

We thank You for Your unfailing love for us that never ends and Your mercies which never cease. Your mercies are new every morning; great is Your faithfulness. We exalt You, our God and King, and we praise Your Name forever and ever. Thank You, Father, for being our strength, our shield, our provider, and our Savior. Thank You for blessing us with jobs that provide us with income. Thank You for promotions and raises. Thank You for favor with our bosses and co-workers.

Praying God's Will

Father, we confess that we will save, spend, and invest money in obedience to Your perfect plan for our lives and our families. We confess that as You bring financial blessings into our lives, we will remember that You give us the power to get wealth. We declare that we are set on high above the nations of the earth because we diligently obey Your voice and carefully observe Your commandments. Father, we confess that all that we set our hands to is blessed because You have commanded blessings on our storehouses, including savings, investments, and retirement accounts. Lord, we declare that, as Your blessings overtake us, we will be able to lend money to many and not have to borrow from anyone. We confess that, as we bring the tithes into Your house, we expect You to pour out blessings so large that we will not have room to receive them. Lord, we declare that we will be faithful stewards of Your financial blessings, and we expect You to confirm Your Word and make us rulers over abundant wealth. We call forth a new anointing of entrepreneurship, new ideas, and new businesses in our communities. Lord, we call forth a spirit of excellence and prosperity in our finances and in all areas of our lives.

Praying for Your Needs

Holy Spirit, help us to shift our focus from spending to saving and from consuming our income to building wealth. We ask You to help us tie loyalty and kindness around our necks and write them deep within our hearts so that we may find favor with both You and people and so that we will earn a good reputation. Father, we pray for promotions and financial increase. Holy Spirit, help us to study the Word, to meditate on it day and night, and to observe to do the things written within it so that we may make our way prosperous and have success in all that we do. Help us to build business and personal relationships with other Christians, and give us favor with the business community. Help us to begin to love people and use money, rather than loving money and using people. We pray for a breaking of old mindsets and generational curses of poverty and lack within our families.

Prayer for Forgiveness

Father, forgive us for our sins. Forgive us for repeating patterns of financial failures, such as living beyond our means and misusing credit cards. Forgive us for failing to develop financial plans that include debt reduction, savings, and investments. Forgive many of us for believing that we are supposed to have the most of the worst and the least of the best. Forgive us for not recognizing that You will not withhold any good thing from us as we walk uprightly before You. Forgive us for words and thoughts of doubt and unbelief. Father, forgive us for walking by sight rather than walking by faith. Lord, remind us of those we need to forgive, and we will be quick to forgive.

Prayer for Protection

Lead us not into temptation; but deliver us from the evil one.

Kingdom Praise and Worship

Lord, You are our Savior. You are the hope of everyone on earth. You formed the mountains by Your power and armed Yourself with mighty strength. You quieted the raging oceans with their pounding waves and silenced the shouting of the nations. Those who live at the ends of the earth stand in awe of Your wonders. From where the sun rises to where it sets, You inspire shouts of joy. In Jesus' name, amen.

Pray to Change Your Life Today

As you can see, The Model Prayer can be applied to any prayer topic. In our prayer classes, we teach students to write out their prayers in order to learn how to apply the model. I want to encourage you to write out your prayers, too. This will help you to become accustomed to the pattern of the model and to think through the intent for the prayer.

There is an old saying, "practice makes perfect." Application is the key to experiencing God's richest blessings through The Model Prayer. The more you practice Jesus' prayer template, the more familiar you will become with its pattern. Take your time and walk through each step of the prayer development. Praying The Model Prayer is not hard. Enjoy your experience and watch the production of God's plans for your life increase exponentially. Begin to change your life today through prayer.

The following exercises are designed to guide you through The Model Prayer and to assist you in developing your prayer. Each exercise consists of a Prayer Development Form, a Prayer Evaluation Form, and a Writing the Prayer Form. Use the Prayer Development Form to develop your prayer. This form contains each section of The Model Prayer with information that will help you to write your prayer. Use the

Scriptures that are listed to compose the paragraphs for Sections 1, 2, and 6. Be careful to adhere to the context of each Scripture. They can be paraphrased, but the Scripture's meaning cannot be altered. I recommend the New Living Translation Bible for writing prayers because it is written in contemporary language, yet its translation is close to the original biblical text. I have written out the Scriptures in Exercise 1 for your convenience. You must look up the Scriptures for Exercise 2 and 3.

The Prayer Evaluation Form contains questions you should ask yourself when fashioning your prayer. It reminds you to include information that is important to the Lord. Write your prayer on the Writing the Prayer Form. Keep the sections in the order they are presented, but feel free to start with any of the sections. After completing your prayer, review the Prayer Evaluation Form one more time. If you answer "no" to any of the questions, then go back and include any information that you may have left out.

Take your time; don't hurry. Remember, the effective, fervent prayers of the righteous have much power. Ask the Holy Spirit to help you. He is very familiar with this model.

Once you have completed your prayer, begin to pray it aloud. Take note of your experience while praying and expect results. I cannot fully explain how this model works, but I know without a doubt that it produces God's results to our prayers.

Exercise 1

Write a prayer for healing using the following Prayer Development Form, Prayer Evaluation Form, and Writing the Prayer Form.

Praying to Change Your Life
Prayer Development Form
Prayer Topic: A Prayer for Healing

Section 1: Intimate Praise and Worship

a. Acknowledge God as Father.

b. Offer thanksgiving (specific to the prayer topic).
c. Lift up adoration and reverence.
   • Psalm 145:1-2
   • Psalm 27:1
   • Isaiah 6:3

Section 2: Praying God's Will

Scriptures should be relevant to the prayer topic.
   • Isaiah 41:10
   • 1 Peter 2:24
   • Psalm 91:14-16

Section 3: Praying for Your Needs

a. What are you asking?
b. Be specific.
c. List your requests:

   • _____

   _____

   • _____

   _____

Section 4: Praying for Forgiveness

a. Ask for forgiveness. (Be specific and list each sin.)

b. Forgive others. (Be specific and name each person.)

c. Forgiveness should be specific to the prayer topic.

d. List your sins and the people you need to forgive:

- _____
  _____
- _____
  _____

Section 5: Praying for Protection
a. *"Lead us not into temptation; but deliver us from the evil one."*
b. Stick with this language unless you are experienced at praying spiritual warfare prayers.
   - Matthew 6:13a

Section 6: Kingdom Praise and Worship
Declare the awesomeness and sovereignty of God.
   - Psalm 86:8-10

Praying to Change Your Life
Prayer Evaluation Form

Section 1: Intimate Praise and Worship
a. Does this paragraph acknowledge God as Father?

Yes   No

b. Is the praise based on Scripture?

Yes   No

c. Are the Scriptures relevant to this section?

Yes   No

d. Do the Scriptures adore and reverence the Lord?

Yes   No

e. Does this section include thanksgiving specific to the topic?

Yes   No

Section 2: Praying God's Will

a. Are the Scriptures appropriate to the prayer topic?

Yes   No

b. Are confession or declaration statements used (Confess, Declare, Decree, Expect)?

Yes   No

Section 3: Praying For Your Needs

a. Are the requests specific to the topic?

Yes   No

Section 4: Praying for Forgiveness

a. Is forgiveness addressed in this paragraph?

Yes   No

b. Is the forgiveness specific to the prayer topic?

Yes   No

c. Did the prayer include forgiving others?

Yes   No

d. Is this forgiveness specific?

Yes   No

Section 5: Praying for Protection

a. Does this paragraph specifically state, *"And do not lead us into temptation; but deliver us from the evil one?"*

Yes   No

Section 6: Praise and Worship

a. Is Scripture used to declare God's sovereignty and awesomeness?

Yes   No

b. Was the paragraph exclusive to God?

Yes   No

c. Will God feel that He has been acknowledged as the only wonderful and great God?

Yes   No

d. Is God glorified?

Yes   No

Praying to Change Your Life
Writing the Prayer Form
Topic: _____

Intimate Praise and Worship

_____

_____

_____

_____

_____

_____

_____

_____

Praying God's Will

_____

_____

_____

_____

_____

_____

_____

_____

Praying for Your Needs

_____

_____

_____

_____

_____

_____

_____

Praying for Forgiveness

_____

_____

_____

_____

_____

_____

_____

Praying for Protection

_____

_____

_____

_____

_____

_____

_____

_____

Kingdom Praise and Worship

_____

_____

_____

_____

_____

_____

NOTE: Appendix G contains a completed prayer using the information on the Prayer Development Form. Your prayer may be different in its articulation, but both prayers should contain the same information.

Exercise 2

Write a prayer for your Finances using the Prayer Development Form, Prayer Evaluation Form, and Writing the Prayer Form.

Praying to Change Your Life
Prayer Development Form
Prayer Topic: A Prayer for Your Finances

Section 1: Intimate Praise and Worship
    a. Acknowledge God as Father.
    b. Offer thanksgiving (specific to the prayer topic).
    c. Lift up adoration and reverence.
- Psalm 96:4-6
- Deuteronomy 8:18

Section 2: Praying God's Will
Scriptures should be relevant to the prayer topic.
- Malachi 3:10-12
- Proverbs 3:9-10

Section 3: Praying for Your Needs
    a. What are you asking?
    b. Be specific.
    c. List your requests:

- _____
  _____
- _____
  _____

Section 4: Praying for Forgiveness
    a. Ask for forgiveness. (Be specific and list each sin.)
    b. Forgive others. (Be specific and name each person.)
    c. Forgiveness should be specific to the prayer topic.

d. List your sins and the people you need to forgive:

- _____

    _____

- _____

    _____

Section 5: Praying for Protection

a. *"Lead us not into temptation; but deliver us from the evil one."*

b. Stick with this language unless you are experienced at praying spiritual warfare prayers.

- Matthew 6:13a

Section 6: Kingdom Praise and Worship

Declare the awesomeness and sovereignty of God.

- 1 Timothy 1:17

Praying to Change Your Life
Prayer Evaluation Form

Section 1: Intimate Praise and Worship

a. Does this paragraph acknowledge God as Father?

Yes   No

b. Is the praise based on Scripture?

Yes   No

c. Are the Scriptures relevant to this section?

Yes   No

d. Do the Scriptures adore and reverence the Lord?

Yes   No

e. Does this section include thanksgiving specific to the topic?

Yes   No

Section 2: Praying God's Will
    a. Are the Scriptures appropriate to the prayer topic?

    Yes   No

    b. Are confession or declaration statements used (Confess, Declare, Decree, Expect)?

    Yes   No

Section 3: Praying For Your Needs
    a. Are the requests specific to the topic?

    Yes   No

Section 4: Praying for Forgiveness
    a. Is forgiveness addressed in this paragraph?

    Yes   No

    b. Is the forgiveness specific to the prayer topic?

    Yes   No

    c. Did the prayer include forgiving others?

    Yes   No

    d. Is this forgiveness specific?

    Yes   No

Section 5: Praying for Protection
    a. Does this paragraph specifically state, *"And do not lead us into temptation; but deliver us from the evil one?"*

    Yes   No

Section 6: Praise and Worship
    a. Is Scripture used to declare God's sovereignty and awesomeness?

    Yes   No

    b. Was the paragraph exclusive to God?

    Yes   No

c. Will God feel that He has been acknowledged as the only wonderful and great God?

Yes   No

d. Is God glorified?

Yes   No

Praying to Change Your Life
Writing the Prayer Form
Topic: _____

Intimate Praise and Worship

_____

_____

_____

_____

_____

_____

_____

_____

Praying God's Will

_____

_____

_____

_____

_____

_____

_____

_____

Praying for Your Needs

_____

_____

_____

_____

_____

_____

_____

Praying for Forgiveness

_____

_____

_____

_____

_____

_____

_____

Praying for Protection

_____

_____

_____

_____

_____

_____

_____

_____

Kingdom Praise and Worship

_____

_____

_____

_____

_____

_____

NOTE: A written prayer is provided in Appendix G.

Exercise 3

Write a prayer for spiritual empowerment using the Prayer Development Form, Prayer Evaluation Form, and Writing the Prayer Form.

Praying to Change Your Life
Prayer Development Form
Prayer Topic: A Prayer for Spiritual Empowerment

Section 1: Intimate Praise and Worship
    a. Acknowledge God as Father.
    b. Offer thanksgiving (specific to the prayer topic).
    c. Lift up adoration and reverence.
       • Psalm 103:1-5

Section 2: Praying God's Will
Scriptures should be relevant to the prayer topic.
    • Philippians 4:13
    • 2 Corinthians 5:21
    • Ephesians 2:10
    • Proverbs 3:5-6
    • 2 Corinthians 5:7
    • Psalm 138:8
    • 1 Corinthians 2:15
    • 2 Timothy 1:7

Section 3: Praying for Your Needs
    a. What are you asking?
    b. Be specific.
    c. List your requests:

       • _____

_____

- _____

_____

Section 4: Praying for Forgiveness
  a. Ask for forgiveness. (Be specific and list each sin.)
  b. Forgive others. (Be specific and name each person.)
  c. Forgiveness should be specific to the prayer topic.
  d. List your sins and the people you need to forgive:

  - _____

  _____

  - _____

  _____

Section 5: Praying for Protection
  a. *"Lead us not into temptation; but deliver us from the evil one."*
  b. Stick with this language unless you are experienced at praying spiritual warfare prayers.
     - Matthew 6:13a

Section 6: Kingdom Praise and Worship
Declare the awesomeness and sovereignty of God.
  - Psalm 89:8-11

Praying to Change Your Life
Prayer Evaluation Form

Section 1: Intimate Praise and Worship
  a. Does this paragraph acknowledge God as Father?

  Yes   No

  b. Is the praise based on Scripture?

  Yes   No

  c. Are the Scriptures relevant to this section?

  Yes   No

    d. Do the Scriptures adore and reverence the Lord?

    Yes   No

    e. Does this section include thanksgiving specific to the topic?

    Yes   No

Section 2: Praying God's Will

    a. Are the Scriptures appropriate to the prayer topic?

    Yes   No

    b. Are confession or declaration statements used (Confess, Declare, Decree, Expect)?

    Yes   No

Section 3: Praying For Your Needs

    a. Are the requests specific to the topic?

    Yes   No

Section 4: Praying for Forgiveness

    a. Is forgiveness addressed in this paragraph?

    Yes   No

    b. Is the forgiveness specific to the prayer topic?

    Yes   No

    c. Did the prayer include forgiving others?

    Yes   No

    d. Is this forgiveness specific?

    Yes   No

Section 5: Praying for Protection

    a. Does this paragraph specifically state, *"And do not lead us into temptation; but deliver us from the evil one?"*

    Yes   No

Section 6: Praise and Worship

    a. Is Scripture used to declare God's sovereignty and awesomeness?

    Yes   No

    b. Was the paragraph exclusive to God?

    Yes   No

    c. Will God feel that He has been acknowledged as the only wonderful and great God?

    Yes   No

    d. Is God glorified?

    Yes   No

Praying to Change Your Life
Writing the Prayer Form

Topic: _____

Intimate Praise and Worship

_____

_____

_____

_____

_____

_____

_____

_____

Praying God's Will

_____

_____

_____

_____

_____

_____

_____

Praying for Your Needs

_____

_____

_____

_____

_____

Praying for Forgiveness

_____

_____

_____

_____

_____

_____

Praying for Protection

_____

_____

_____

_____

_____

_____

_____

Kingdom Praise and Worship

_____

_____

_____

_____

_____

_____

NOTE: A written prayer for spiritual empowerment is provided in Appendix G.

CHAPTER 9

PRAY-ERS WITH MOUNTAIN-MOVING FAITH

For what is faith unless it is to believe
what you do not see?
—St. Augustine

God has provided everything we need to partner with Him to achieve His plans on the earth. The Lord has given us prayer, the supernatural vehicle that enables us to communicate for Him. He has given us His Word, which acts as the power source of that prayer vehicle. He has given us a pattern through The Model Prayer that gives us a clear and orderly blueprint for our communications.

We have everything we need, right?

Not quite. Prayer, the vehicle, is in position. The Word, which is the prayer battery and payload, is working. The prayer model, or frame, is sound. Yet, we can't start the vehicle until we have the key.

Thankfully, God gives us that too. The key is *faith*. Without it, powerful, productive prayers are impossible. With it, Mark 11:23 says that we can move mountains!

What is faith? Hebrews 11:1 says, *"Faith is the substance of things hoped for, the evidence of things not seen."* This definition indicates that faith is not based upon any evidence our physical senses can provide.

Paul parallels this truth in Second Corinthians 5:7 saying: *"We walk by faith, not by sight."* Sight is related to the physical world: the realm of material, temporary, and changeable things. Faith, however, is based on the eternal, unchanging, and invisible truths and realities revealed by God's Word. Faith requires a sense of perception within our spirits that can see into the supernatural and behold the great and mighty things God has in store for us.

Faith is the key that unlocks the supernatural and releases the spiritual things of God. The Greek word for faith is *pistis*,[1] which means the conviction of truthfulness. The Truth of God is His Word. If faith is Truth-centered, it must be Word-centered.

You may have heard Christians say, "That Word really convicted me," or "The pastor's sermon convicted me today." Conviction occurs when Truth is revealed. We have already learned that God's Word has a purpose—to teach, to reprove, to correct, to instruct, and to reveal. The conviction that Christians experience results from the Word carrying out its purpose.

One person may be convicted to forgive someone. Another may be convicted to repent for something or to start doing something or even to praise God. These responses reveal the presence of faith. This faith, which is fueled by the conviction Truth brings, always puts the Word into action. Therefore, faith enables the purpose of the Word to prevail.

God's Faithfulness

As humans, it is hard for us to always keep the faith. We may give it a good try, but inevitably, even with the best of intentions and often in circumstances beyond our control, we sometimes fall short.

God knows us and has reasonable expectations of us. His Word never says that we are faithful, that our spouses are faithful, that our jobs are faithful, that material items are faithful. Instead, the Word says that God is faithful:

> *God is faithful, by whom you were called into the fellowship of His Son, Jesus Christ our Lord.*[2]

> *No temptation has overtaken you except such as is common to man; but God is faithful, who will not allow you to be tempted beyond what you are able, but with the temptation will also make the way of escape, that you may be able to bear it.*[3]

> *But the Lord is faithful, who will establish you and guard you from the evil one.*[4]

God is the only One who cannot lie. He is the only One who is able to keep every promise He has made. He is the only One who never sleeps nor slumbers and whose thoughts are many toward each of us. He is the only One who can save and heal us. He is the only One who is completely faithful.

Mark 11:22 states: *"Have faith in God."* When we do not believe, our unbelief does not change who He is. When we do not take Him at His Word, His Word does not change. Because His very nature is faithfulness, we can have and know faith through Him, despite our human inconsistencies.

The Origin of Our Faith

Faith is not something fabricated by man. Even in those moments when our faith seems unshakeable, we must remind ourselves that our faith does not originate with us. Faith begins and ends with Jesus:

> *Looking unto Jesus, the author and finisher of our faith, who for the joy that was set before Him endured the cross, despising*

the shame, and has sat down at the right hand of the throne of God.[5]

Jesus began the faith walk for us. Philippians 2:6-8 describes Him as *"being in the form of God,"* in fact *"equal with God."* Yet, Paul explains that Jesus *"made Himself of no reputation, taking the form of a bondservant and coming* [to earth] *in the likeness of men.... He humbled Himself and* [was] *obedient to the point of death, even the death of the cross."* Because of His obedient actions, our faith is made perfect. Through Christ, we can see the invisible realm and expect the completion of things hoped for.

Jesus showed us how faith and the Word go hand in hand. Throughout the Scriptures, He did one thing before He did anything else—He prayed to His Father for instructions. Once He heard the Word of God, He acted upon it.

Jesus didn't leave His "prayer closet," run to tell His disciples what His Father said to do, and then procrastinate about doing it. He didn't sit on a rock mulling over what His Father said, only to decide the time wasn't right to obey God's instruction.

Instead, Jesus faithfully acted upon God's Word—and He gave us the opportunity to follow His lead. He was completely convinced of the Father's Truth, never doubting its probity. In John 12:50, we see that Jesus spoke what the Father said, knowing that the results would be eternal in nature: *"And I know that His command is everlasting life. Therefore, whatever I speak, just as the Father has told Me, so I speak."*

The Keys to Faith

Jesus provided for us the example of perfected faith. The following keys help us to understand the kind of faith that Jesus had. But, it is also important to understand that faith does not end with Jesus; He provided for us to be able to walk in it.

As the following passages show, the Bible contains numerous examples of individuals who internalized and actualized a strong, mountain-moving faith in order that God's will would be done on earth. In documenting their lives, these Scriptures also illustrate three important faith keys.

1. Faith is supported and sustained by the Word of God.

"Now therefore, behold, the cry of the children of Israel has come to Me, and I have also seen the oppression with which the Egyptians oppress them. Come now, therefore, and I will send you to Pharaoh that you may bring My people, the children of Israel, out of Egypt." But Moses said to God, "Who am I that I should go to Pharaoh, and that I should bring the children of Israel out of Egypt?" So He said, "I will certainly be with you. And this shall be a sign to you that I have sent you; when you have brought the people out of Egypt, you shall serve God on this mountain." Then Moses said to God, "Indeed, when I come to the children of Israel and say to them, 'The God of your fathers has sent me to you,' and they say unto me 'What is His name?' what shall I say to them?" And God said to Moses, "I AM WHO I AM." And He said, "Thus shall you say to the children of Israel, 'I AM has sent me to you.'"[6]

Afterward Moses and Aaron went in and told Pharaoh, "Thus says the Lord God of Israel; 'Let My people go that they may hold a feast to me in the wilderness.'" And Pharaoh said, "Who is the Lord, that I should obey His voice to let Israel go? I do not know the Lord, nor will I let Israel go."[7]

And the Lord spoke to Moses, saying, "Go in, tell Pharaoh, king of Egypt to let the children of Israel go out of his land." And Moses spoke before the Lord saying, "The children of Israel have not heeded me. How then shall Pharaoh heed me, for I am of circumcised lips?" Then the Lord spoke to Moses and Aaron, and gave them a command for the children of Israel and for Pharaoh king of Egypt, to bring the children of Israel out of the land of Egypt.[8]

And the Lord spoke to Moses, "Go to Pharaoh and say to him, 'Thus says the Lord: "Let My people go, that they may serve Me. But, if you refuse to let them go, behold I will smite all your territory with frogs."'"… And the Lord said to Moses, "Rise early in the morning and stand before Pharaoh as he comes out to the water. Then say to him, 'Thus says the Lord: "Let My people go that they may serve Me. Or else, if you will not let My people go, behold, I will send swarms of flies on you and your servants, on your people and into your houses. The houses of the Egyptians shall be full of swarms of flies, and also the ground on which they stand."'"[9]

So Moses and Aaron came in to Pharaoh and said to him, "Thus says the Lord God of the Hebrews: 'How long will you refuse to humble yourself before Me? Let My people go, that they may serve Me. Or else, if you refuse to let My people go, behold, tomorrow I will bring locusts into your territory'."[10]

Moses was able to go before Pharaoh, time after time, and repeat God's warnings because he knew he had heard from God. Moses' faith continued, even when it looked as though Pharaoh would never relent.

Despite the king's rebellion and refusal to obey, Moses chose to follow what God told him to do every time. Because of Moses' faith, the children of Israel were delivered in a mighty way.

2. Faith always obeys the Word of God.

By faith Noah, being divinely warned of things not yet seen, moved with godly fear, prepared an ark for the saving of his household, by which he condemned the world and became heir of the righteousness which is according to faith.[11]

Noah believed the Word of God, and because of his obedience, not only were he and his household saved, but the salvation of the entire world was enacted through him. Abraham's obedience was equally powerful in bringing God's will to pass:

By faith Abraham obeyed when he was called to go out to the place which he would receive as an inheritance. And he went out, not knowing where he was going. By faith he dwelt in the land of promise as in a foreign country, dwelling in tents with Isaac and Jacob, the heirs with him of the same promise; for he waited for the city which has foundations, whose builder and maker is God.[12]

Abraham left where he had lived his entire life because God told him to. Before God spoke to him, Abraham didn't even believe in God! He wasn't raised in a godly home; he didn't know anything about the Lord, but when God spoke, he obeyed. Because he chose to believe and obey, all the nations of the world have been blessed.

Moses, Noah, Abraham, and others were people of action. This is a godly trait; James 1:22-25 explains that having faith dictates that we must be not only hearers of the Word, but doers also.

James warns the person who is a hearer only, saying *"He is like a man observing his natural face in a mirror; for he observes himself, goes away, and immediately forgets what kind of man he was"* (verses 23-24). The passage goes on to promise the doer that he will be blessed in what he does.

3. Faith trusts God, even in the face of death.

Daniel 3:10-26 relays the story of three young Jewish exiles—Shadrach, Meshach, and Abednego—who refused to worship the king of Babylon's gold statue or to serve any of his gods.

When the king threatened to throw the men into a fiery furnace as punishment for their disobedience to his decrees, their response was firm in faith:

> *If that is the case, our God whom we serve is able to deliver us from the burning fiery furnace, and He will deliver us from your hand, O king. But if not, let it be known to you, O king, that we do not serve your gods, nor will we worship the gold image which you have set up.*[13]

The three men were bound and thrown into the fiery furnace, which had been heated seven times hotter than usual. To the king's amazement, the three men were not consumed by the fire. Instead, unbound and unharmed, they walked around in the flames and were joined by a fourth person who looked like a divine being.

The king shouted to the men to come out and all three stepped out of the furnace, showing no signs of being in the fire. The king praised their God, decreed that no one was to speak a word against Him, and promoted them to higher positions in the province of Babylon.

Even in the face of death, the men did not deny God. Their faith and trust were greater than their desire to survive. They knew that God had the power to deliver them, but they didn't know for sure that He would. We can't second-guess the Lord, but we can trust that He is God and that His greatness, His awesomeness, His power, and His love will never change.

Many of us may think that we could not attain to a level of faith that would enable us to obey God at all costs and even choose death over life. Others of us have experienced such tremendous pain in our lives that our faith has been shattered, and we do not believe that it can ever be recovered.

Be encouraged. God has not left us alone to do what is humanly impossible. He sent us His Son in whose perfect faith our faith can be completed. He sent us the Holy Spirit, our Counselor who abides in us forever and applies the truth of God to our hearts. And He sent us direction through His Word. *"So then faith comes by hearing, and hearing by the word of God."*[14]

In the ancient Jewish tradition, it was the practice of the Hebrew people to speak or recite the Word of God, what we now call the Old Testament. That was how the Word was passed down from generation to generation for hundreds of years.

This was a people who understood the power of the spoken Word. They also understood that God's Word alone does not produce faith but that the hearing of God's Word does. The faith it produces gives us access to all that God provides, from our daily bread to the gift of salvation.

In Him you also trusted, after you heard the word of truth, the gospel of your salvation; in whom also, having believed, you were sealed with the Holy Spirit of promise.[15]

Did you know that hearing God's Word renews your mind? Did you also know that hearing what is contrary to God's Word fills your mind—and your life—with darkness?

The question becomes: what have you been listening to? What have you been tuning into day after day? What ongoing messages are you allowing to come into your mind and take root? Are you speaking into your children, your spouse, your friends the negative words that may have been spoken into your life—that you are not good enough, that you are not smart enough, that you will never be enough?

You can make the decision to turn away from the spoken words that are limiting your faith in God and in yourself. Romans 12:2 says that your mind can be renewed and your life transformed by God's Word:

> *Do not be conformed to this world, but be transformed by the renewing of your mind, that you may prove what is that good and acceptable and perfect will of God.*

In John 15:7, the Lord instructs us to abide in Him and in His Word. When we do so, He promises that we will *"ask what we desire and it shall be done for us."*

As we listen to God's Word, it brings us power. As we speak God's Word, its purpose is fulfilled in us; our faith grows bolder, and our trust in God becomes stronger than any circumstance or fear. Our faith becomes our shield, protecting us from the *"fiery darts of the wicked one"* and anything that comes against us—even death.

Mountain-moving faith comes by hearing the Word of God, believing what He says, and acting upon His principles and commands. When we declare His Word aloud, it speaks to us and communicates God's intentions. It consoles us when we are discouraged; it strengthens us when are weak; it corrects us when we have made a mistake; it applauds us when we have triumphed.

In the first chapter of Luke, Mary is visited by an angel and told that she would give birth to the Son of the Most High. What was Mary's answer to this astonishing news? "Let it be to me according to your word."[16] And the Christ Child was born. By faith, Mary was able to set herself in agreement with God's plan.

> *But, without faith it is impossible to please Him, for he who comes to God must believe that He is, and that He is a rewarder of those who diligently seek Him.*[17]

Imagine this dramatic scenario: your life is in danger and you hear of someone who has the power and the means to save your life.

Now, imagine yourself approaching this person, not with confidence in his ability, but doubting that he could provide the life-saving gift you need. Although you sought him out, the only real reason you were there was because someone told you to go.

You acknowledge having heard some good things about this person, but you never bothered to check out the story: you didn't talk to his references or familiarize yourself with his credentials. You didn't follow through because you did not really believe that he was whom he claimed to be. The bottom line is: you didn't believe he could deliver.

Faith that moves mountains and produces God's plans on earth does not approach situations in this half-hearted way. Mountain-moving faith is proactive; it does not waiver or dwell in uncertainty. Romans 14:23 warns us that the person *"who doubts is condemned if he eats, because he does not eat from faith; for whatever is not from faith is sin."*

When questions arise, mountain-moving faith will drive you to find Truth, which will, in turn, produce action. James 1:5-6 tells us that, anytime we lack wisdom for a situation, we can ask God for it, and He will give it to us freely—provided we ask in faith without doubting.

Faith propels us toward God in anticipation of sweet communion with Him and in confidence in His willingness to provide what we need. Faith is the key that unlocks every spiritual promise of God.

Faith is grounded in the belief that God *is*. In this book, we have touched on His character and characteristics, His make-up and His attributes. We've gone to His Word and followed His model, and still, we have not come close to describing His glory. When we believe all that God is, we position ourselves to please Him and to be rewarded for our belief and our faith.

The greater our faith, the greater the reward. Believe that God is the Healer, and He will heal you. Believe that He is a Sustainer, and He will sustain you. Believe that He will protect you and your family as you sleep, and He will. Believe that He will wake you up in the morning, and you can count on it. God waits for our belief and faith to draw us closer to Him.

Praying in Faith

Praying The Model Prayer requires the faith to believe and accept it as God's pattern for advancing His Kingdom on earth.

I have been asked, "Do we have to pray this way?" My question in response is, "Why wouldn't we pray this way?" First, Jesus instructed us to use The Model Prayer. Second, it is the only model presented by Jesus. Third, what do we have to lose by using it?

It is The Kingdom Prayer for Kingdom living. It is comprehensive in its scope, and it clearly expresses God's yearning for relationship with humanity. Furthermore, it creates a partnership and guarantees great benefit. Praying The Model Prayer produces what God wants for humanity; in return, we are provided for abundantly.

Praying through The Model Prayer, using the sections as our guide, releases God's power and authority in us to be the people He has created us to be and to do the things He has called us to do.

As a result, we become agents of change. We can do all things in Christ; we can speak to mountains, and they will move; we can lay hands on the sick, and they will recover; we can rebuke demons, and they will flee.

As you pray using The Model Prayer, expect your communications to move Heaven and earth. Above all, expect your relationship with

God to grow from mere acquaintanceship to powerful friendship, as it did in Abraham's life:

> *And the Scripture was fulfilled which says, "Abraham believed God, and it was accounted to him for righteousness* [because of his faith].*" And he was called the friend of God.*[18]

Expect a sweetness and a confidence from thanking and praising God, attending to His business, lifting up requests, asking for forgiveness, praying for protection, and glorifying His greatness. Expect your faith to move mountains!

CHAPTER 10

Prayer and Results

Success…is not often gained by direct effort as by careful, systematic, thorough preparation for duty.
—George S. Boutwell

Empowered to Pray

When we began this journey together, I promised you that it would accomplish two things: one, you would understand why we are called to pray, and two, you would know what to say when you pray. You can judge best the level of success we have attained.

Most of the material in this book is based on a series of prayer classes that I, along with a team of instructors, have had the privilege to teach over the years.

In every first class, the seats are filled with people from all backgrounds and levels of faith. A few have some experience with prayer and want to find out how they can incorporate our teachings on The Model Prayer.

Most, however, are individuals who consider themselves inadequate and intimidated pray-ers. I am always grateful for the opportunity to see each person's growth in confidence and faith over the course of the classes—particularly in the case of those individuals who begin the class with obvious uncertainty about their ability to pray.

I am humbled that God has given me the assignment to arm His people with the tools to produce prayers that get results. And now, through this book, you have those tools too.

It does not matter where you were in your prayer life when you started reading this book or where you are now. What matters is this: if you apply what the Lord has given me to share with you and if you invest time in the Word and in practice of The Model Prayer, then you will witness answered prayers beyond your expectations—sometimes in the form of miracles. I have provided a prayer guide containing prayers on a variety of topics in Appendix H for practice. Pray these prayers and practice learning Jesus' model for praying. Psalm 77:14 states: *"You are the God who does wonders; You have declared Your strength among the peoples."* You are equipped as God's vessel to pave the way for God's wonders—through prayer.

Answered Prayers

Over and over again, I have seen the Lord work His wonders through this model of prayer. I would like to share some of the results experienced by people who are using The Model Prayer. Their testimonies are told in their own words.

As a result of my experience with the Kingdom Builders' Prayer Institute, God has given me a boldness to pray for anyone, anytime, anywhere. I have also seen "evidence" of healing, miracles, and breakthroughs as a result of my prayers for myself and others. Prayer has become such an integral part of my life that, like American Express, "I don't leave home without it."

—M. Grafenreed

As a member of the Windsor Village United Methodist Church Prayer Ministry, I learned to pray The Model Prayer under the instruction of Pastor Suzette Caldwell.

I use the model to pray directly for members of the congregation and during personal prayer time. Utilizing the model that Jesus gave His disciples adds an extra layer of faith to my prayers because I know that I'm addressing a given topic the way the Lord wants it addressed. I'm mindful that Scripture contains numerous examples of Jesus praying before achieving many significant milestones. Miracles, signs, and wonders followed Jesus' prayers, so I enthusiastically heed His instruction in Matthew 6:9, "In this manner, therefore, pray."

I have witnessed the power and effectiveness of praying model prayers in Jesus' name on many occasions. In some cases, with immediate results and at other times, I have received praise reports later. I walk and pray in absolute confidence that God will answer my prayers because I know that I have followed the Lord's recipe, so the prayer has to produce good results that will bring Him glory and bless His people.

During the years I have prayed The Model Prayer, God has blessed my family richly. Some of His answered prayers have included amazing healings including the healing of:

- Major medical ailments in the brain of my stepfather

- Heart conditions in my mother and stepfather

- My uncle's HIV

The Lord also kept one of my grandchildren in the womb for 38½ weeks after my daughter-in-law had bouts of premature labor at 17 and 25 weeks. He has also restored relationships with family members that have been fractured for 20 years. He has delivered other members of my family from drug addiction. God has brought forth a substantial increase in our financial storehouses through promotions, investments, and unexpected income streams.

The Word of the Lord is true—the effective, fervent prayers of the righteous avail much, especially when we pray using His model."

—F. LeBlanc

Learning how to pray using The Model Prayer was a revelation for me. It taught me how to pray effective and powerful prayers that did not return to me void.

As we went through each of the sections of The Model Prayer, I learned a lot about myself and why I may not have received the results that I was seeking from God because of the way that I had been praying. I had been starting off the prayer with complaining and not taking the time to say "Hello" to God.

I came to know God as my Father. I could come before Him in love, giving Him thanks for all that He says He is to me. I learned to adore Him, to take time to love Him. I no longer compared God to my earthly situation. Once I took time to let Him know how much He meant to me, I could remind Him of His Word, which I found out was His will for me. I could speak exactly what He had written and expect Him to act upon His Word. I did not have to beg or be repetitious or demanding. I found that His Word was the truth and that He was true to His Word. If I was obedient to His Word, and applied His Word to my circumstances, His will would be manifested in my life.

When I would get to the part about praying for my needs, I learned that I really did not have any "needs." I had already spoken what God said about my situation, and it took care of my needs. I found God to be gracious and caring and realized that He still wanted me to express the desires of my heart.

After learning to pray according to The Model Prayer, I found myself praying for the needs of others more than I prayed for myself. My prayers were no longer "selfish." Praying according to The Model Prayer took the focus off me, and I began to focus more on what God wanted to accomplish for the day or a particular topic.

Growing up, I never took the time to stop and allow the Holy Spirit to show me myself. One of the best things about seeking forgiveness from my Father is that, once it is done, I do not have to allow the enemy to use the past against me. I can hold my head up and have no shame.

I love what God is doing in me in the area of unforgiveness. I found that I have to forgive as I desire my Father to forgive me. This I found to be a process, but God is patient with me, and I am able to forgive and let go. It is very cleansing. I have had the best blood pressure results in a very long time—to the point where my doctor has started taking me off some medication. God is good!

When I get to Section 5, I know that when I say, "Do not lead us into temptation, but deliver us from the evil one," that God is protecting me and my family. He has become my shelter and my way of escape.

In closing out the prayer praising God for His sovereignty, I am assured that my family and I are covered. I know that we are citizens in God's Kingdom, and in God's Kingdom, it is His responsibility to take care of His citizens.

I would tell anyone who wants to know how to pray effective and powerful prayers to simply pray as Jesus taught His disciples by praying The Model Prayer.

—G. Scott

I thank God for the Kingdom Builders' Prayer Institute. Because of the classes, I believe my prayers are hitting the mark.

A few months ago, God placed it on my family's heart to move. I prayed and asked God to bless the entire process. We prepared our house to be sold. When we put it on the market, it was fewer than 10 days before we had five buyers, including one who wanted to pay more than the list price.

Before we moved, I called an insurance agent to get a quote on our homeowner's insurance for the new house. I told the man that we had sold our house and were getting ready to move into a new house. I shared with him what God had done for us; he was amazed. He said that the house that he was selling had been on the market for months and that, when he did get an offer, it wasn't worth a hill of beans.

Before I hung up, I asked him if he believed in Jesus. He said he did and that he had asked Him to help sell his house. I said, "Well God is no respecter of persons and the same thing He did for me, He will do for you."

I proceeded to ask him if I could pray for him and ask God to do the same thing for him. He answered, "Yes."

The following day, I called the man to confirm the quote he had given me on my house. He said, "Hey, I told my wife I was going to call you. Yesterday, I received an offer for my house, and it was the amount I was asking for."

To God be the glory!

—N. Jones

I am so thankful for the prayer class. I have seen some improvements in my health, finances, and the employment I have been seeking is coming forth, in Jesus' name.

—K. Grappie

When I think about how praying according to The Model Prayer has influenced and had an effect on my life, I have to begin with how my understanding of how to pray has changed.

Before, when I prayed, I must confess that I was often redundant, praying only for the desires that concerned my family, close friends, situations in my life, or anything that involved or revolved around my own existence.

Whenever anyone asked me to pray for them, I'd say, "Yes, of course, I'll pray." I would pray whatever I thought was needed in a generic way to help those in need, and I hoped that I had prayed appropriately.

As a result of learning how to pray the model that Jesus taught His disciples to pray, I have experienced a closer relationship with God as Father. I acknowledge Him in a way that allows me to feel a closeness to Him, offering up to Him praise and worship before I begin listing any concerns or needs that exist. This has taught me more about reverence and thanksgiving when going before the throne of grace.

Learning to pray according to God's will has opened up and enlightened my understanding of the power that exists when I pray according to the Word of God. My relationship with God the Father has deepened as a result of praying the Word and learning how to find Scripture that relates to cares, concerns, desires, and needs.

My prayer language has become more bold and distinct as a result of searching the Word to pray God's will. Learning and understanding the importance of searching my heart when asking for forgiveness has truly helped me to be less self-centered and more aware of the importance of asking forgiveness for specific sins and transgressions. It has also helped me to forgive others and to keep no record of offenses.

Praying according to The Model Prayer has given me a deeper understanding of who God is as my heavenly Father, and has given me a closer relationship with Him than I have ever experienced before.

Much in my life has changed and is changing because my prayer life is more focused and illuminated. For me, every opportunity now to pray is a deeper, more personal, and broadening experience.

—T. Wright

Not long after I started attending Windsor, I heard about The Prayer Institute. I began attending the classes and my life hasn't been the same since. It was exactly where I needed to be. I learned so much from God's Word, and God used the class in such a way to deal with everything I was experiencing. It was almost as if I had been placed on an operating table and God used your words to dissect my heart and get to the root of my condition—unforgiveness.

The forgiveness aspect of the prayer model was so key in my liberation. It began the healing process. I became hungry for God, His Word, His will, and His way.

—I. Rodriguez

I was a student of the prayer class a few years back. I had been unable to hear in my left ear for about 18 months. The doctors said that there was bone formation in the ear, causing loss of hearing.

I and the gentleman who prayed for me went to the front of the class. You instructed him to place his fingers in my ear and begin to pray. I heard a pop and felt a warm sensation in my ear. I was able to hear immediately. You asked if I could hear you. I told you I could hear you. You asked if I could hear you clearly. I said, "Yes, I can hear you clearly."

I can still hear clearly. I completed the prayer class and have found that I am no longer afraid to pray because I know how to pray. I thank God for you and for the Kingdom Builder's Prayer Institute."

—M. Gee

When I walk into a room of familiar people, people who have not seen me for a while, or even people who have just met me for the first time, I get the same response: "You look good."

My familiar friends have been wondering what I have done to enhance or change my look. They have been probing me about the amount of rest I am getting, the meals I have been eating, or the physician I have been seeing.

When time permits, I tell them, "This is the new me...the praying me, the steadfast me, the faithful me, the standing-on-the-Word-of-God me!"

I visited Windsor Village for six years, and during that time, I was able to collect enough knowledge to understand that there was something powerful in the prayer Jesus taught His disciples. Before Pastor Suzette's teachings about The Model Prayer, all I knew to pray was my laundry list of begging and pleading and what I needed in life and wanted out of life at that moment. I moved from my agenda, which produced little or no results, to just simply praying the prayer that Jesus presented in the Word of God.

Praying The Model Prayer saved me from a life of divorce, depression, anxiety, and literally death. You see, I had the two-story home, the six figure income, the husband, the 2.5 children and the SUV to go with it all. This is what I was taught to ask for…financial increase, prosperity, and material blessings.

I was used to asking from God, and I got what I asked for. But those things were nothing that an education and a good job couldn't get on their own! I was missing all the elements to make me a peaceful, productive asset to the Kingdom of God. I was missing the "…on earth as it is in Heaven" mission I was to live out right now.

I have successfully completed Prayer 101 and 102, and my life has not been the same. I now walk in authority, bringing the Kingdom of God with me. Knowing the Word of God, studying the Word of God, and searching what the Word has to say about every situation enables me to pray The Model Prayer effectively. It has kept me peaceful and prosperous. The automatic peace that comes with praying God's Word is priceless.

I still have the home, income, husband, and now three children; but more importantly, I have the peace of God that gives me the authority to walk into a room and light it up! I thank God for His faithfulness and for covering me in my ignorance of prayer.

—A. Taylor

In One Accord

In addition to serving as Chairman of the Kingdom Builders' Prayer Institute, I am an Associate Pastor and a founding member of the prayer ministry for Windsor Village United Methodist Church in Houston, Texas. My husband, Kirbyjon Caldwell, has served as Senior Pastor of Windsor for more than 25 years.

For the majority of that time, my husband has led the Windsor Village Church Family in addressing the unmet needs of people in the historically under-served and under-developed area where the church is located.

As a result, more than 100 ministries, as well as several individually managed nonprofit organizations and community development projects, have been realized to improve the lives of God's people.

Many of these projects have been prayed into existence by groups of people—determined prayer partners standing shoulder to shoulder with faithful church members—all armed with written prayers loaded with the Word of God and based on the prayer that Jesus taught His disciples. In some cases, the prayer groups have prayed to prevent certain projects or circumstances from taking root. The following two testimonies demonstrate how praying The Model Prayer has resulted in the rebirth of a community and in the harnessing of a hurricane.

A Community Revitalized

There is no limit to what prayer can accomplish in your personal life, your family, your community, or even your world. Allow me to share a wonderful testimony to God's provision and faithfulness; it beautifully demonstrates the power of The Model Prayer.

Mr. Donald Bonham, the now deceased former owner of Fiesta Mart, Inc., posed a question to my husband: "If you could do anything you wanted with 24 acres of land, an 86,000-square-foot abandoned Kmart building, and a 5,000-square-foot auto parts store, what would you do?"

My husband did not answer immediately, but told Mr. Bonham he would get back with him. A few days later, while shopping in a 24-hour Super Wal-Mart in Jonesboro, Arkansas, God gave my husband the answer to Mr. Bonham's question.

Kirbyjon and I were visiting my mother and doing some shopping for her. While browsing throughout the store, God dropped the vision for the 24 acres of land and two buildings into my husband's heart.

The vision was to create a one-stop complex of social services to meet the needs of the people in the surrounding community. While Wal-Mart offered an array of goods, this facility would provide an array of social and spiritual services under one roof.

The vision was cast before the church congregation and a prayer strategy was developed to make this vision into an earthly reality. If we were to experience this divine vision, we were going to have to use divine methods. Our supernatural activities included prayer-walking the buildings and property, holding scheduled prayer times, fasting, and declaring God's Word.

Prior to the beginning of construction activities, we held a ring of prayer. More than 600 people formed a ring around the old Kmart building and prayed using a written prayer filled with God's Word.

At this time in our history, approximately 1996, I was just beginning to teach about The Model Prayer. I did not yet fully understand its phenomenal power. This prayer did not include all sections of The Model Prayer, but as I learned more about the significance of the prayer pattern, subsequent prayers were modified to incorporate it in its entirety.

Over time I would come to learn more about The Model Prayer's extraordinary properties. But this event marked a prayer milestone— the start of writing prayers to unite the congregation.

Because the level of faith or spiritual maturity of all the believers was not known, a prayer was written to even the playing field and reduce the risk of anyone praying in doubt and unbelief.

Together, we sang songs of praise and then prayed the prayer. United, we prayed aloud, in faith, and with the confidence of knowing that our prayers would accomplish God's will for the vision. Throughout the years, we continued to pray using The Model Prayer as our guide.

The once vacant Kmart store is now The Power Center, a 21st century model of public and private partnership that includes a Chase Bank branch; a private family healthcare office; a pharmacy and optical center; a Women, Infants and Children's program office; a hair salon; a school; real estate development offices; Entrepreneurial Power Suites (low-cost office space with shared services); and the Jesse H. Jones Conference Center. The Power Center provides employment for 230 people, serves more than 11,000 families per month, and generates $15 million in economic activity annually.

Since the construction of The Power Center, a 234-acre mini master-planned community has been developed. This project includes a 462-home, affordably priced, quality residential subdivision called Corinthian Pointe, which is completely occupied by many families who are first-time homeowners.

Corinthian Pointe was built in three phases. Each phase sold out before it was completed. Each of the 462 homes is brick; amenities such as trees, garages, and sidewalks have contributed to increases in property values. Collectively, the households in Corinthian Pointe spend $16.5 million per year, and generate an additional $8.6 million in economic impact. In addition, since Corinthian Pointe was built, other residential projects have added to the revitalization of the area.

Diligently, over a six-year period, we prayed for the Corinthian Pointe development using The Model Prayer format. Believers gathered weekly on the once undeveloped property and commanded those things which do not exist as though they did.[1] Our prayers covered all involved parties: the bankers, builders, contractors, architects, and city officials. We spoke to each phase of the Corinthian Pointe project, expecting godly results.

We then turned our attention to another of God's visions. In September 2007, across the street from Corinthian Pointe, the doors of the Kingdom Builders' Family Life Center were opened. The Center, comprising 191,000 square feet, provides educational, recreational, social, financial, and spiritual programs and services to children, youth, adults, and families.

The master-planned community also includes a commercial tract consisting of Walgreens, CVS, and McDonald's stores; The Texas Children's Pediatrics Practice for children; an assisted living complex for seniors; and a retail shopping center.

The Model Prayer is the spiritual catalyst for the marvelous things God is doing through this tremendous project. To date, we continue to pray using The Model Prayer concerning Phase II, which will consist of a new church sanctuary, an office building, and the crown jewel of the entire project—The Prayer Center. The Prayer Center will provide worship, training, and prayer services 24 hours a day, 7 days a week.

Is there anything too hard for God? No!

A Testimony About Hurricane Rita

On September 24, 2005, Houston was threatened by what was the third most intense storm in history up to that point—Hurricane Rita. Rita was forecasted to wreck devastation within the Galveston Gulf Coast region and the Houston metropolitan area. Houstonians were encouraged to evacuate. Over one million people attempted to leave, creating massive gridlock and gas and water shortages.

Approximately 72 hours before Rita was scheduled to make landfall, I was retiring for the night. While saying my prayers, I heard the Holy Spirit say, "Write a prayer to address the concerns about Hurricane Rita."

I was very tired and ready to go to sleep. I responded by saying, "Now, Lord? I am so tired I just want to go to sleep. May I write the prayer in the morning?" I heard the Holy Spirit say clearly, "If you wait until the morning, several key hours will have passed."

I thought about this for a couple of minutes and decided to get up and write the prayer. I called a partner of our church's prayer ministry and asked her if she would help me compose the prayer and put it online to our network of intercessors. She agreed immediately to help. We wrote the prayer using The Model Prayer format and sent it out that night.

While writing the prayer, I wondered if we were crazy to think that our praying could influence the weather. Then I remembered the story of Jesus speaking peace to the storm and telling it to be still. I decided to trust God's instruction to write the prayer.

I based our actions on Ephesians 5:1: *"Imitate God, therefore, in everything you do, because you are His dear children"* (NLT). If Jesus spoke to the storm, then we would follow His example and speak to Hurricane Rita.

I am told that the prayer spread throughout the city. A local radio station picked it up and began to encourage its listeners to use the prayer. Later, after the impending danger had passed, I received word that the prayer had spread as far as California. This prayer united the city and enabled us to pray the same prayer, the same way, on the same day.

Let me pause here and say that there is power in united prayer. In Acts 2:1-2, on the Day of Pentecost, the people of God were in one place praying in one accord and suddenly the Holy Spirit appeared. We needed a *suddenly* moment in Houston. United prayer caused that moment to occur.

Seemingly at the 11th hour, Hurricane Rita took an unexpected turn and headed in a different direction. On the day that it was expected to devastate Houston, the sun came out and a small amount of rain showered the northern quadrant of Houston.

Did the prayer have anything to do with Hurricane Rita's sudden change? Yes, I believe this without a doubt. Below is a copy of the instructions and prayer that the citizens of the Greater Houston area prayed concerning Hurricane Rita.

Dear Believer,

Stand in your front or backyard, extend your hand in the direction of the Gulf of Mexico and speak to Hurricane Rita.

Pray with the authority that has been given to you in Jesus Christ, and pray in faith. Please pray this prayer out loud with fervency and determination. God has placed His power in our verbal expressions, so lift up your voice. Believe that your prayers will produce results in Jesus' name.

Please pray this prayer one or two times per day.

Thank you, in advance, for standing on the wall for the Houston Metropolitan area.

Below is the actual prayer text that was distributed throughout the Greater Houston area and elsewhere:

Prayer Against Hurricane Rita

Father, there is none like You. You are great and Your name is great in might. Who would not fear You, O King of the nations? This is Your rightful due. Among all the wise men of the nations and in all their kingdoms there is none like You.

We acknowledge You as Lord over the United States. Thank You for blessing our great city. Thank You for Your continued love, grace, and provision.

Using the authority given to us in the name of Jesus, we speak to Hurricane Rita, and we command the winds and storms to dissipate. We command the peace of God to be still within Hurricane Rita, and we declare that Rita will not bring harm or devastation to Houston and the surrounding coastal areas.

Lord, we ask You to touch the heart of every believer in this area to pray against this hurricane. Father, please forgive us for our many sins. Please forgive disobedience, rebellion, unbelief, forms of idolatry, shedding of innocent blood, and the rejection of Your Son, Jesus Christ. God have mercy on the Houston metropolitan area.

Lord, help us to overcome our temptations and deliver us from this impending destruction.

We ask You to destroy every satanic assignment against us.

Now to You, the King Eternal, Immortal, Invisible, to You who alone is wise, be honor and glory forever and ever. In Jesus' name, amen.

Called to Pray

The Lord is calling all of us to pray. Like the loving Almighty Father that He is, He has made provision for us to do that which He calls us to do. He is the same God who, as Isaiah 42:5 tells us, *"created the heavens and stretched them out."* He is the One who created the earth and everything in it, and He gives breath to everyone who walks the earth.

The same God created The Model Prayer. It is for everyone to use, including you. Be encouraged by the Word, which shows us how God has used the prayers of men and women to advance His Kingdom for centuries.

Be encouraged by the testimonies of 21st century men and women whose prayers are being used by God to achieve His will on the earth right now.

Be encouraged that the Lord loves us enough to send His Word to defeat cancer, debt, loneliness, stress, unemployment, poverty, hopelessness, confusion, despair, or anything that would separate us from Him or prevent us from being effective for His Kingdom.

Prayer works. Prayer based on The Model Prayer produces powerful results. You can do this. Start now! Go online to www. prayerinstitute.com, download our monthly prayer guide, and join believers around the world in unified prayer to pray for God's will. I call it The Power Guide. It serves as a powerful tool for accomplishing God's will on earth. Every month, believers around the world enter into unified prayer by praying the same prayer, the same way (every prayer is written using The Model Prayer pattern), on the same day. According to Acts 2:1, when the disciples were in one accord, "suddenly" the Holy Spirit fell upon them. I believe that this type of unified prayer, using the Power Guide, will create more "suddenly" moments on earth. Picture God's Word rising from the earth as thick as smoke every day because of united prayer. I don't know about you, but that makes me excited!

Finally, allow me to leave you with a prayer written especially for you. I invite you to pray this prayer aloud and expect God to change your life.

The Believer's Prayer of Victory

Father, You are great and most worthy of praise. No one can measure Your greatness. Lord, the earth is Yours and everything in it; the world and all its people belong to You. You are King! You are robed in majesty and armed in strength. The world stands firm and cannot be shaken. Your throne has stood from time immemorial. You Yourself are from the everlasting past. I thank You for Your unconditional love. Thank You for protecting me and providing for me. Thank You for all of the blessings that You have bestowed on my life.

Father, I confess that I can do all things through Christ who strengthens me. I am like a tree planted by the rivers of water, and I will produce fruit in my season. My leaves will never wither, and I will prosper in all that I do. I was made for Your good pleasure, and I have complete confidence that wherever I go and whatever I do will be blessed.

Holy Spirit, please help me to pray in the way that Jesus instructed. Help me to trust God with all of my heart, mind, soul, and strength. Father, teach me how to become Your partner through prayer.

Forgive me for my sins. Forgive me for [confess any sins that you have committed]. Father, in order for me to receive Your forgiveness, I must be forgiving. Right now, I make the choice to forgive. [Ask the Holy Spirit to show you the faces or names of those people who you have not yet forgiven and list them here.]

Do not lead me into temptation, but deliver me from the evil one.

To You, the King eternal, immortal, invisible, the only wise God—be honor and glory forever and ever. In Jesus' name, amen.[2]

APPENDIX A

PRAYERS OF PRAISE
AND PERSONAL CONFESSION

Prayer of Praise

Scriptural Prayer (from Psalm 95:1-5)

Today I come to sing to You, Lord! I shout joyfully to the Rock of my salvation. I come before Your presence with thanksgiving; I shout joyfully to You with psalms. For You are the great God and the great King above all gods. In Your hands are the deep places of the earth; the heights of the hills are Yours also. The sea is Yours, for You made it; and Your hands formed the dry land.

(See Chapter 4, Exercise 1.)

Biblical Confession About the Believer

Scriptural Prayer (from Psalm 92:12-15)

As the righteous, I shall flourish like a palm tree. I shall grow like a cedar in Lebanon. I am planted in the house of the Lord, and I shall flourish in the courts of my God. I shall bear fruit in my old age; I shall be fresh (fat) *and flourishing* (green), *and I shall declare that the Lord is upright; He is my rock, and there is no unrighteousness in Him.*

(See Chapter 4, Exercise 2.)

Declaration of God's Will for Successful Living (from Psalm 1)

Scripture Passage

Blessed is the man who walks not in the counsel of the ungodly, nor stands in the path of sinners, nor sits in the seat of the scornful; but his delight is in the law of the Lord, and in His law he meditates day and night. He shall be like a tree planted by the rivers of water, that brings its fruit in its season, whose leaf also shall not wither; and whatever he does shall prosper. The godly are not so, but are like the chaff which the wind drives away. Therefore the ungodly shall not stand in the judgment, nor sinners in the congregation of the righteous. For the Lord knows the way of the righteous, but the way of the ungodly shall perish.

Scriptural Prayer

I am blessed and I will not walk in the counsel of the ungodly, nor stand in the path of sinners, nor sit in the seat of the scornful. My delight is in the law of the Lord, and I will meditate on His law day and night. I shall be like a tree planted by the rivers of water that brings forth its fruit in its season, whose leaf also shall not wither. Whatever I do shall prosper. It is not so for the ungodly. They are like chaff which the wind drives away. Therefore the ungodly shall not stand in the judgment, nor sinners in the congregation of the righteous. The Lord knows my way because I am the righteous. But, the way of the ungodly shall perish.

(See Chapter 4, Exercise 3.)

APPENDIX B

PRAYERS OF PRAISE AND FAMILY BLESSING

Prayer of Praise

Scriptural Prayer (from Psalm 111:2-7 NLT)

Father, Your deeds are amazing! All who delight in You should ponder them. Everything You do reveals Your glory and majesty. Your righteousness never fails. You cause us to remember Your wonderful works. You are gracious and merciful. You give food to those of us who fear You; You always remember Your covenant. You have shown Your great power to Your people by giving them the lands of other nations. All You do is just and good and all Your commandments are trustworthy.

(See Chapter 5, Exercise 1.)

Prayer of Blessings for the Family

Scriptural Prayer (from Psalm 128)

I am blessed because I fear the Lord and walk in His ways. When I eat the labor of my hands, I shall be happy and it shall be well with me. My spouse shall be like a fruitful vine in the very heart of my house, my children will be like olive plants all around my table. Behold, I shall be blessed because I fear the Lord. Lord, bless me out of Zion, and I will see the good of Jerusalem all the days of my life. Yes, I will see my children's children. Peace be upon Israel.

(See Chapter 6, Exercise 1.)

APPENDIX C

PRAYERS OF PRAISE

The following scriptural prayers are taken (with paraphrasing in some cases) from the Scriptures listed at the beginning of each. Where needed, the prayers were personalized so that you can speak your praises directly to God.

Speak these prayers out loud and with passion. Infuse these words with your love and excitement for God. He will enjoy hearing your affection toward Him.

Prayer from 1 Chronicles 29:10-13

Blessed are You, Lord God of Israel, our Father, forever and ever. Yours, O Lord, is the greatness, the power, the glory, the victory and the majesty; for all that is in heaven and in earth is Yours; Yours is the kingdom, O Lord and You are exalted as head over all. Both riches and honor come from You, and You reign over all. In Your hand is power and might; in Your hand it is to make great and to give strength to all. Now therefore, our God, we thank You and praise Your glorious name.

Prayer from Nehemiah 9:6 NLT

You alone are the Lord. You made the skies and the heavens and all the stars. You made the earth and the seas and everything in them. You preserve and give life to everything, and all the angels of heaven worship You.

Prayer from Psalm 89:5-8 NLT

All heaven will praise Your miracles, Lord; myriads of angels will praise You for Your faithfulness. Who in all of heaven can compare with You, Lord? What mightiest angel is anything like You? The highest angelic powers stand in awe of You. You are far more awesome than those who surround Your throne, O Lord God Almighty! Where is there anyone as mighty as You, Lord? Faithfulness is Your very character.

Prayer from Revelation 4:11 NLT

You are worthy, O Lord our God, to receive glory and honor and power. You created everything, and it is for Your pleasure that they exist and were created.

Prayer from Revelation 15:3-4 NLT

Great and marvelous are Your actions, Lord God Almighty. Just and true are Your ways, King of the nations. Who will not fear, O Lord, and glorify Your name? For You alone are Holy. All nations will come and worship before You, for Your righteous deeds have been revealed.

Prayer from Isaiah 6:3 NLT

Holy, Holy, Holy is the Lord Almighty; the whole earth is filled with His glory!

Prayer from Psalm 97:1-9 NLT

Lord, You are King! Let the earth rejoice! Let the farthest coast-lands be glad. Clouds and darkness surround You. Righteousness and justice are the foundation of Your throne. Fire goes forth before You and burns up all Your foes. Your lightning flashes out across the world. The earth sees and trembles. The mountains melt like wax before You, the Lord of all the earth. The heavens declare Your righteousness; every nation sees Your glory. Those who worship idols are disgraced—all who brag about their worthless gods—for every god must bow to You. Jerusalem has heard and rejoiced, and all the cities of Judah are glad because of Your justice, Lord! For You, O Lord, are most high over all the earth; You are exalted far above all gods.

Prayer from Psalm 99:1-3 NLT

Lord, You are King! Let the nations tremble! Lord, You sit on Your throne between the cherubim. Let the whole earth quake! Lord, You sit in majesty in Jerusalem, supreme above all the nations. Let them praise Your great and awesome name. Your name is holy!

Prayer from Psalm 24:7-10 NLT

Open up, ancient gates! Open up, ancient doors, and let the King of glory enter. Who is the King of glory? The Lord, strong and mighty; the Lord, invincible in battle. Open up, ancient gates! Open up, ancient doors, and let the King of glory enter. Who is the King of glory? The Lord Almighty—He is the King of glory.

Prayer from 1 Timothy 6:15-16

To You, who is the blessed and only Potentate, the King of kings and Lord of lords, who alone has immortality, dwelling in unap-proachable light, whom no man has seen or can see, to whom be honor and everlasting power. Amen.

Prayer from Psalm 95:3-6 NLT

Lord, You are a great God, the great King above all gods. You own the depths of the earth. The mightiest mountains are Yours. The sea belongs to You, for You made it. Your hands formed the dry land, too. Come, let us worship and bow down. Let us kneel before the Lord our maker.

APPENDIX D

Prayer Exercises—Protection, Gratitude, and Spiritual Power

In the following exercises, read the Scripture passages provided. Then proceed to the scriptural prayers and fill in the blanks to personalize them.

Exercise 1: Prayer for Protection (from Psalm 91:1-7)

Scripture Passage

He who dwells in the secret place of the Most High shall abide under the shadow of the Almighty. I will say of the Lord, "He is my refuge and my fortress; my God, in Him I will trust." Surely, He shall deliver you from the snare of the fowler and from the perilous pestilence. He shall cover you with His feathers, and under His wings you shall take refuge; His truth shall be your shield and buckler. You shall not be afraid of the terror by night, nor of the arrow that flies by day, nor of the pestilence that walks in darkness, nor of the destruction that lays waste at noonday. A thousand may fall at your side, and ten thousand at your right hand; but it shall not come near you.

Scriptural Prayer

_____ *will dwell in the secret place of the Most High and* _____ *shall abide under the shadow of the Almighty.* _____ *say of the Lord, "He is my refuge and my fortress; my God, in Him I will trust." Surely, He shall deliver* _____ *from the snare of the fowler and from the perilous pestilence. He shall cover* _____ *with His feathers, and under His wings* _____ *shall take refuge; His truth shall be* _____ *shield and buckler.* _____ *shall not be afraid of the terror by night, nor of the arrow that flies by day, nor of the pestilence that walks in darkness, nor of the destruction that lays waste at noonday. A thousand may fall at* _____ *side, and ten thousand at* _____ *right hand; but it shall not come near* _____ .

(See Appendix F for the completed version of this prayer.)

Exercise 2: Prayer of Gratitude for God's Provision (from Psalm 103:1-5)

In this exercise, personalize the Scripture passage to form a prayer in which you speak directly to God.

Scripture Passage

Bless the Lord, O my soul; and all that is within me, bless His holy name! Bless the Lord, O my soul, and forget not all of His benefits: who forgives all your iniquities, who heals all your diseases, who redeems your life from destruction, who crowns you with loving-kindness and tender mercies, who satisfies your mouth with good things, so that your youth is renewed like the eagle's.

Scriptural Prayer

_____ *bless* _____ *Lord, with all of* _____ *soul and all that is within* _____ , _____ *bless* _____ *holy name!* _____ *bless* _____ ,

Lord and _____ will not forget all of _____ benefits. _____ have forgiven all of _____ iniquities and healed all of _____ diseases. _____ have redeemed _____ from destruction and crowned _____ with loving-kindness and tender mercies. _____ satisfy _____ mouth with good things, so that _____ youth is renewed like the eagle's.

(See Appendix F for the completed version of this prayer.)

Exercise 3: Prayer for Spiritual Power (from Isaiah 61:1-2 NLT)

Scripture Passage

The Spirit of the Sovereign Lord is upon Me, for the Lord has anointed Me to bring good news to the poor. He has sent Me to comfort the brokenhearted and to proclaim that captives will be released and prisoners will be freed. He has sent Me to tell those who mourn that the time of the Lord's favor has come, and with it, the day of God's anger against their enemies.

Scriptural Prayer

The Spirit of the Sovereign Lord is upon _____, for the Lord has anointed _____ to bring good news to the poor. He has sent _____ to comfort the brokenhearted and to proclaim that captives will be released and prisoners will be freed. He has sent _____ to tell those who mourn that the time of the Lord's favor has come, and with it, the day of God's anger against their enemies.

(See Appendix F for the completed version of this prayer.)

PRAYERS OF PRAISE AND ADORATION

Prayer of Praise and Adoration (from Psalm 89:5-8 NLT)

Scripture Passage

All heaven will praise Your great wonders, Lord; myriads of angels will praise You for Your faithfulness. For who in all of heaven can compare with the Lord? What mightiest angel is anything like the Lord? The highest angelic powers stand in awe of God. He is far more awesome than all who surround His throne. O Lord God of Heaven's Armies! Where is there anyone as mighty as You, O Lord? You are entirely faithful.

Scriptural Prayer

All heaven will praise Your great wonders, Lord; myriads of angels will praise You for Your faithfulness. For who in all of heaven can compare with <u>You</u>, Lord? What mightiest angel is anything like <u>You</u>? The highest angelic powers stand in awe of <u>You</u>. <u>You</u> are far more awesome than all who surround <u>Your</u> throne. O Lord God *of Heaven's Armies! Where is there any as mighty as <u>You</u>, O Lord? <u>You</u> are entirely faithful.*

(See Chapter 7, Exercise 1.)

Prayer of Praise and Adoration (from Jeremiah 10:12-16 NLT)

Scripture Passage

But God made the earth by His power, and He preserves it by His wisdom. With His own understanding He stretched out the heavens. When He speaks in the thunder, the heavens roar with rain. He causes the clouds to rise over the earth. He sends the lightning with the rain and releases the wind from His storehouses. The whole human race is foolish and has no knowledge! The craftsmen are disgraced by the idols they make, for their carefully shaped works are a fraud. These idols have no breath or power. Idols are worthless; they are ridiculous lies! On the day of reckoning they will all be destroyed. But the God of Israel is no idol! He is the Creator of everything that exists, including Israel, His own special possession. The Lord of Heaven's Armies is His name!

Scriptural Prayer

God, you made the earth by Your power, and <u>You</u> preserve it by <u>Your</u> wisdom. With <u>Your</u> own understanding <u>You</u> stretched out the heavens. When <u>You</u> speak in the thunder, the heavens roar with rain. <u>You</u> cause the clouds to rise over the earth. <u>You</u> send the lightning with the rain and release the wind from <u>Your</u> storehouses. The whole human race is foolish and has no knowledge! The craftsmen are disgraced by the idols they make, for their carefully shaped works are a fraud. These idols have no breath or power. Idols are worthless; they are ridiculous lies! On the day of reckoning they will all be destroyed. But, <u>You</u>, God of Israel, are no idol! <u>You</u> are the Creator of everything that exists, including

Israel, <u>Your</u> own special possession. The Lord of Heaven's Armies is <u>Your</u> name!

(See Chapter 7, Exercise 1.)

Completed Prayers of Protection, Gratitude, and Spiritual Power

Prayer for Protection

Scriptural Prayer (from Psalm 91:1-7)

I will dwell in the secret place of the Most High and I shall abide under the shadow of the Almighty. I say of the Lord, "He is my refuge and my fortress; my God, in Him I will trust." Surely, He shall deliver me from the snare of the fowler and from the perilous pestilence. He shall cover me with His feathers and under His wings I shall take refuge; His truth shall be my shield and buckler. I shall not be afraid of the terror by night, nor of the arrow that flies by day, nor of the pestilence that walks in darkness, nor of the destruction that lays waste at noonday. A thousand may fall at my side, and ten thousand at my right hand; but it shall not come near me.

(See Appendix D, Exercise 1.)

Prayer of Gratitude for God's Provision

Scriptural Prayer (from Psalm 103:1-3)

I bless You, Lord, with all of my soul and all that is within me, I bless Your holy name! I bless You, Lord, and I will not forget all of Your benefits. You have forgiven all of my iniquities and healed all of my diseases. You have redeemed me from destruction and crowned me with loving-kindness and tender mercies. You satisfy my mouth with good things, so that my youth is renewed like the eagle's.

(See Appendix D, Exercise 2.)

Prayer for Spiritual Power

Scriptural Prayer (from Isaiah 61:1-2 NLT)

The Spirit of the Sovereign Lord is upon me, for the Lord has anointed me to bring good news to the poor. He has sent me to comfort the brokenhearted and to proclaim that captives will be released and prisoners will be freed. He has sent me to tell those who mourn that the time of the Lord's favor has come, and with it, the day of God's anger against their enemies.

(See Appendix D, Exercise 3.)

APPENDIX G

COMPLETED PRAYERS OF HEALING, FINANCES, AND SPIRITUAL EMPOWERMENT

These prayers refer back to the exercises at the end of Chapter 8, "Walk the Talk." There you wrote out prayers of Healing, Finances, and Spiritual Empowerment using the Prayer Development Form, Prayer Evaluation Form, and Writing the Prayer Form.

Your prayers may be different in articulation, but both your prayers and these provided here should contain the same information. In these prayers, the sections for Praying for Your Needs and Praying for Forgiveness are somewhat generic. But you will want to make sure that your prayers reference your *specific* needs, the sins you need forgiveness for, and the people you need to forgive.

The Scriptures in the first two prayers are taken from the New Living Translation. The third prayer contains Scripture from both the New King James Version and the New Living Translation.

Exercise 1: A Prayer for Healing

Section 1: Intimate Praise and Worship (from Psalm 145:1-2, Psalm 27:1, and Isaiah 6:3)

Heavenly Father, I exalt you. You are my God and King and I will praise Your name forever and ever. I will praise You every day; yes, I will praise You forever. You are great, Lord! You are most worthy of praise! No one can measure Your greatness. You are my light and my salvation, so why should I be afraid? You are my fortress protecting me from danger, so why should I tremble? Holy, holy, holy is the Lord of Heaven's Armies! The whole earth is filled with His glory! Thank You for blessing my family. Thank You for your grace and mercy. Thank You for the food that we eat and the clothes that we wear.

Section 2: Praying God's Will (from Isaiah 41:10, 1 Peter 2:24, Psalm 91:14-16)

Today, I will not be afraid, for You are with me. I confess that I will not be discouraged, for You are my God. Wonderful Father, You are my strength and my help, and I know that You will uphold me with Your victorious right hand. You personally carried my sins in Your body on the cross so that I could be dead to sin and live for what is right. By Your wounds, I am healed. I declare that no weapon formed against me will prosper. Lord, Your Word says that You will rescue me because I love You, and You will protect me because I trust in Your name. You said that You would answer me when I called You and be with me when I am in trouble. You promised to rescue and honor me, reward me with a long life, and give me Your salvation. By faith, I stand on Your Word, and I decree healing in my body now!

Section 3: Praying for Your Needs

Holy Spirit, help me to walk by faith. Help me to laugh more and enjoy every day to its fullness. Remind me to stand on God's Word daily.

Section 4: Praying for Forgiveness

Father, forgive me for doubt and unbelief. Forgive me for not taking care of my health. Forgive me for all of my sins. Holy Spirit, remind me of who I need to forgive, and help me to forgive.

Section 5: Praying for Protection (from Matthew 6:13a)

Lead me not into temptation; but deliver me from the evil one.

Section 6: Kingdom Praise and Worship (from Psalm 86:8-10)

No pagan god is like you, O Lord; none can do what you do! All the nations you made will come and bow before you, Lord; they will praise Your holy name. You are great and perform wonderful deeds. You alone are God. In Jesus' name, amen.

Exercise 2: A Prayer for Your Finances

Section 1: Intimate Praise and Worship (from Psalm 96:4-6, Deuteronomy 8:18)

Gracious Father, You are great and most worthy of praise! You are to be feared above all gods. The gods of other nations are mere idols, but You made the heavens! Honor and majesty surround You; strength and beauty fill Your sanctuary. Thank you for blessing me with employment. Thank you for helping me to finish my project at work. Thank you for giving me favor with my colleagues.

Holy Spirit, thank You for giving me the power to get wealth so that Your covenant is established.

Section 2: Praying God's Will (from Malachi 3:10-12, Proverbs 3:9-10)

Holy Father, You said to bring all of the tithes into the storehouse so that there is enough food in Your Temple. I am a tither [if you are not a tither, commit to adhering to this Scripture so that you may enjoy its promises], and as a result, I am expecting You to pour out a blessing so great from the windows of Heaven that I will not have enough room to take it in! You said to tithe and to put You to the test! By faith, I decree that my crops will be abundant and protected from insects and disease. My grapes will not fall from the vine before they are ripe, and all nations will call me blessed, for my land will be such a delight.

Section 3: Praying for Your Needs

Holy Spirit, help me to trust God's Word concerning my finances. Please bless me with a $10,000 increase in my income. Give me creative ideas for obtaining wealth, and send people and resources to help me achieve my goals.

Section 4: Praying for Forgiveness

Righteous Father, forgive me for not trusting You with my finances. Forgive me for not being a good steward of the finances and assets that You have provided for me. Forgive me for being stingy or greedy. Holy Spirit, remind me of anyone that I need to forgive concerning my finances and help me to be quick to forgive.

Section 5: Praying for Protection (from Matthew 6:13a)

Lead me not into temptation; but deliver me from the evil one.

Section 6: Kingdom Praise and Worship (from 1 Timothy 1:17)

All honor and glory to You, God, forever and ever! You are the eternal King, the unseen one who never dies; You alone are God. In Jesus' name, amen.

Exercise 3: A Prayer for Spiritual Power

Section 1: Intimate Praise and Worship (from Psalm 103:1-5)

Father, let all that I am praise You; with my whole heart, I will praise Your holy name. Let all that I am praise You, Lord. I will never forget the good things You do for me. You have forgiven all my sins and healed all my diseases. You redeemed me from death and crowned me with love and tender mercies. You have filled my life with good things and renewed my youth like the eagle's. Jesus, thank You for providing me with salvation and eternal life. Holy Spirit, thank You for leading and guiding me.

Section 2: Praying God's Will (from Philippians 4:13, 2 Corinthians 5:21, Ephesians 2:10, 2 Corinthians 5:7, Proverbs 3:5-6, Psalm 138:8, 1 Corinthians 2:15, 2 Timothy 1:7)

Today, I declare that I can do all things through Christ who strengthens me. I am the righteousness of God. I am His masterpiece, and I have been created anew in Christ Jesus so that I can do the good things He planned for me long ago. I confess that I walk by faith and not by sight. I will trust in the Lord with all my heart, and I will not depend on my own understanding. I will seek God's will in all that I do, and He will show me which path to take. The Lord will work out His plans for my life—for His faithful love endures forever. I will never be abandoned by the

Lord because He made me. I have the mind of Christ, therefore, I can think like Him, act like Him, talk like Him, walk like Him, and believe like Him. God has not given me a spirit of fear, but I have His Spirit of power, love, and a sound mind.

Section 3: Praying for Your Needs

Holy Spirit, please help me to walk in the fullness of the Word that I have declared in my life today. Strengthen my self-esteem and place your confidence within me. Continue to lead and guide my life. Help me to rest in You.

Section 4: Praying for Forgiveness

Lord, forgive me for not embracing the new person I became when I accepted Jesus Christ as my Lord and Savior. Forgive me for saying and doing things that did not align with Your Word. Forgive me for unbelief and doubt.

Section 5: Praying for Protection (from Matthew 6:13a)

Lead me not into temptation; but deliver me from the evil one.

Section 6: Kingdom Praise and Worship (from Psalm 89:8-11)

O Lord, God of Heaven's Armies, where is there anyone as mighty as You? You are entirely faithful. You rule the oceans and subdue the storm-tossed waves. You crushed the great sea monster and scattered Your enemies with Your mighty arm. The heavens are Yours, and the earth is Yours. In Jesus' name, amen.

APPENDIX H

POWER PRAYER GUIDE

Contents

A Prayer for Forgiveness and Forgiving Others
A Prayer for Physical Healing
A Prayer for Mental Healing
A Prayer for Business Leaders
A Prayer for the United States Elections
A Prayer for the Economic Crisis in the United States of America
Prayer Expectations

Dear Brothers and Sisters in Christ,

Prayer is the key to accomplishing God's plans. When we pray in accordance with His Word, we pray His will. The prayers listed in this Prayer Guide are based on God's Word. As you pray them, allow His Word to minister to you.

Isaiah 55:11 states that God's Word does not return to Him empty, but it will accomplish what God wants for our lives, and it will always produce fruit. Pray these prayers out loud. The power of God's Word is activated when we speak it out loud. Lastly, expect results. Expect God's plans concerning each prayer petition to become earthly realities.

Thank you for reading *Praying to Change Your Life*. I look forward to hearing about your encounters with God as you pray using The Model Prayer.

God bless you!
Pastor Suzette Caldwell

How to Use Your Power Prayer Guide

*Now this is the confidence that we have in Him, that if we ask
anything according to His will, He hears us. And if we know
that He hears us, whatever we ask, we know that we have the
petitions that we have asked of Him.*

—1 John 5:14-15

The Power Guide is designed as a tool for study, reflection, and prayer. In order to maximize the use of your guide, please follow the listed instructions.

1. Spend your prayer time praying individually, with your family or prayer partner(s) for at least one hour.

2. Refer to the Prayer Petition Calendar for the specific prayer petition for the day. Allow at least 30 to 60 minutes for you to read and meditate on the Scriptures provided in the daily Scripture reading, and pray the scriptural prayer.

3. Trust the Holy Spirit to help you to expand upon the prayers. Use the prayers as a springboard to openly communicate with the Lord. If you speak in tongues, please pray in tongues over each prayer petition. Relax, listen, and enjoy the Lord.

4. Record any reflections, revelations, or inspiration in the Prayer Expectation section on the last page of the booklet.

5. Believe that the Lord is hearing your prayer, and know in your heart that your praying will produce results.

6. Enjoy your time spent with the Lord.

Prayer Petition Calendar
(Sample)

Sunday	Monday	Tuesday	Wednesday	Thursday	Friday	Saturday
1 Petition 1	2 Petition 2	3 Petition 3	4 Petition 4	5 Petition 5	6 Petition 6	7 Petition 7
8 Petition 8	9 Petition 9	10 Petition 10	11 Petition 11	12 Petition 12	13 Petition 13	14 Petition 14
15 Petition 15	16 Petition 1	17 Petition 2	18 Petition 3	19 Petition 4	20 Petition 5	21 Petition 6
22 Petition 7	23 Petition 8	24 Petition 9	25 Petition 10	26 Petition 11	27 Petition 12	28 Petition 13
29 Petition 14	30 Petition 15					

Prayer Petition 1: A Prayer of Adoration and Reverence for God and His Word

Scripture Reading: Psalm 148, Deuteronomy 6:1-9

Reflections of the Heart

Our God is an awesome God. He is kind, tenderhearted, and merciful. Our Father loves us with an everlasting love and He is always concerned about our welfare. All that we need, He provides through Jesus Christ and the Holy Spirit. God should always be revered and adored. He should have our utmost respect. Today, bless the Lord. Lift up your praises to the One who is the living God, our God who is our Father.

Scriptural Prayer

Father, today we proclaim Your Name, the Name of the Lord. You are glorious. You are our Rock, and Your deeds are perfect. Everything You do is just and fair. You are faithful, and You do no wrong. How just and upright You are! Your unfailing love toward those who fear You is as great as the height of the heavens above the earth. Let the whole world fear and stand in awe of You, Lord. You spoke and the world began; it appeared at Your command. Lord, You are our inheritance and hope. Thank You, Father, for Your love and compassion. Thank You for keeping Your covenant with us throughout the ages. Thank You for making us Your people. What a joy it is to be one of Your children. Father, You are good and Your faithful love endures forever.

Father, today, we reverence and honor You. You are our God, and we submit our loyalty and adoration to You. You are the Alpha and Omega, the beginning and the end. You existed before time and created everything that exists. We acknowledge that You are the only living God. There are no other gods. Father, You are compassionate and merciful, slow to get angry, and filled with unfailing love. You are good to everyone, and You shower compassion on all of Your creation. All of Your works will thank You, Lord, and we, Your followers, praise You. You are so awesome! We confess that we will keep Your commandments, walk in Your ways, and revere You. Father, we confess that Your instructions are perfect, reviving our souls. Your decrees are trustworthy, making wise the simple. Your commandments are right, bringing joy to our hearts. Your commands are clear, giving insight for living. Revering You is pure, lasting forever. Your laws are true, and each one is fair. Father, Your Word is more desirable than gold, yes, even the finest gold. Your Word is sweeter than honey dripping from the honeycomb. Your Word warns us, and we expect great reward as we adhere to it. Father, You are great and greatly to be praised. We will bless You at all times and constantly speak of Your praises.

Father, please let Your ears be attentive to our prayer. Holy Spirit, teach us how to reverence and adore our Father in true holiness. Please touch the hearts of those who do not reverence and adore You, and help them to love You with all their hearts, souls, and strength. Holy Spirit, place in us a hunger and thirst for Your righteousness so that we will be filled.

Father, forgive us for sins of pride, rebellion, disobedience, selfishness, hatred, and idolatry. Lord, forgive us for half-hearted worship. Forgive us for disrespecting Your name and treating You irreverently. Forgive those of us who are parents for not teaching our children to revere and adore You. Lord, remind us of those we need to forgive; and help us to forgive.

Lead us not into temptation; but deliver us from the evil one.

You are God alone; there is no other God and there never has been and there never will be. You are the Lord and there is no other

Savior. From eternity to eternity, You alone are God. All honor and glory belongs to You forever and ever! You are the eternal King, the unseen One who never dies; You alone are God. Yours is the Kingdom and the power and the glory forever. In Jesus' Name, amen.

Scripture References for the Written Text

Deuteronomy 32:3-4, Psalm 103:11, Psalm 33:8-9, Lamentations 3:24, Psalm 136:1, Revelation 1:8, Psalm 145:8-10, Deuteronomy 8:6, Psalm 19:7-10, Psalm 96:4, Psalm 34:1, Deuteronomy 6:5, Matthew 5:6, Matthew 6:13, Isaiah 43:10-11,13, 1 Timothy 1:17

Today, I will trust God to:

_____

_____

_____

_____

_____

_____

_____

_____

Prayer Petition 2: A Prayer for Our Family Members, Friends, Co-workers and Enemies Who Have Not Accepted Jesus Christ as Their Lord and Savior

Scripture Reading: Psalm 84, John 3:1-21

Reflections of the Heart

Isn't it good to know that God saves us by His special favor when we believe? Salvation is a gift from God, so we cannot take credit for it.

Salvation is not a reward for the good things we have done, therefore, none of us can boast about it.

Scriptural Prayer

O Lord, our God, Your majestic name fills the earth. Your glory is higher than the heavens. Our souls bless You, and we will remember the good things You have done for us. You are the One who forgives all our sins, heals us from diseases, redeems us from death, and crowns us with love and tender mercies. You fill our lives with good things and renew our youth like the eagle's! We honor You as our Lord and Savior. Thank You for the gift of salvation through Your Son, Jesus Christ. We thank You for extending Your unfailing love toward us. Thank You, Father, for the tremendous harvest of souls in our city. You are great and deserving of all praise.

Father, it is Your will that prayers, intercessions, and thanksgiving be made for all men so that we can live peaceful and quiet lives marked by godliness and dignity. It is Your desire that all men be saved and understand the truth that You are the only God and that there is only one Mediator who can reconcile humanity back to You—the man, Jesus Christ. Today, we acknowledge that Jesus Christ is the way, the truth, and the life. He is the only door by which people can be saved. Father, You are so rich in kindness and grace that You have purchased our freedom with the blood of Jesus Christ, Your Son, and have forgiven our sins. We declare, by faith, that [list names of nonbelievers] will confess with their mouths that Jesus is Lord and believe in their hearts that God raised Jesus from the dead, and we expect that they will be saved. Father, we decree that they will know the truth, and the truth will set them free. As for me, I confess my sins. I believe that You are faithful and just to forgive me of my sins and to cleanse me from all unrighteousness. I submit to You, my spirit, soul, and body.

Father, we ask You to clear the way so that Your Gospel may be preached in [name of your city]. *As You know, the harvest is great. Please send laborers to proclaim Your Word of salvation to* [list names of nonbelievers]. *Holy Spirit, stir up their hearts and remove the darkness that keeps them from seeing and receiving You. As Your Word goes forth, Holy Spirit, please touch their hearts to receive Your gift of salvation. Holy Spirit, touch the hearts of believers, who have strayed away from You, to return to You and Your eternal love. Father, use me as an answer to this prayer and give me Your courage and boldness to witness Your love and salvation to nonbelievers.*

Father, forgive [list the names of nonbelievers] *for not acknowledging You and receiving Your Son. Forgive them for all acts of sinfulness, including disobedience, hatred, rebellion, murder, idolatry, homosexuality, greed, racism, adultery, fornication, injustice, and violence. Please have mercy upon them and extend Your grace toward them. Forgive those believers who have strayed from You. Forgive us, the Body of Christ in* [name of your city], *for not sharing Jesus and the Gospel with more people. Forgive me for being timid and reserved about sharing the Gospel. Lord, remind all of us of those persons we need to forgive, and please help us to forgive.*

Lead all of us not into temptation; but deliver us from the evil one.

Lord, You alone have held the oceans in Your hand. You measured off the heavens with Your fingers. Only You know the weight of the earth and have weighed the mountains and hills on a scale. All the nations of the world are but a drop in the bucket to You;

they are nothing more than dust on the scales. You pick up the whole earth as though it were a grain of sand. The Lord God Almighty is Your name. In Jesus' name, amen.

Scripture References for the Written Text

Psalm 8:1, Psalm 103:2-3, 1 Timothy 2:1-2, 4-5, John 14:6, John 10:9, Ephesians 1:7, Romans 10:9, John 8:32, 1 John 1:9, Luke 10:2, Matthew 6:13, Isaiah 40:12,15

Today, I will trust God to:

_____

_____

_____

_____

_____

_____

_____

_____

Prayer Petition 3: A Prayer for the Construction of a New Church or New Building

Scripture Reading: 1 Chronicles 16:8-16, Nehemiah 3

Reflections of the Heart:

The God of Heaven Himself will help us succeed; therefore, we will arise and build! We will trust His Word and believe in the Sovereign Lord who always keeps His promises. (See Nehemiah 2:20.)

Scriptural Prayer

Father, we thank You for Your faithful love for us that never ends and Your mercy which never ceases. They are new every morning; great is Your faithfulness. Lord, You are God. You created the heavens and earth and put everything in place. You made the world to be lived in, not to be a place of empty chaos. You are the Lord, and there is no other. You publicly proclaim bold promises; You do not whisper obscurities in dark corners. We thank You for giving our leaders the vision to build. Thank You for providing the resources for us to build. Thank You, Father, for being a wall of fire and protection around our congregation, families, and those involved in the construction of this new building.

Father, we command that Your Kingdom come and Your will be done on earth as it is in Heaven for the construction of the [name the facility] project. We believe that You will make our thoughts agreeable to Your will so that the plans for this project may be established and succeed. Your Word, Father, declares that for lack of advice, plans go wrong; but with many advisers there is success. Therefore, we confess that we will seek the counsel of the godly as we proceed with this project. We declare that we will write the vision for this new project plainly so that those involved can run and carry the correct message to others. Father, we expect You to call forth competent and skilled laborers for this project, just as You called forth the artisans for the building of the tabernacle. We confess that they will be filled with the Spirit of wisdom, understanding, and knowledge in all manner of workmanship. We proclaim that all involved in this project will focus their attention and efforts so that they can successfully complete their assignments and bring glory and honor to Your name. Father, we are confident that the new facility will be completed, because You have begun this good work. Lord, I commit to praying without ceasing for this project.

Father, please bless this new building project to provide activities for our Church Family and the families in the community that will promote growth, development, relaxation, and enjoyment. Please provide all of the wisdom, finances, and resources that we will need to build a state-of-the-art facility. We ask You to provide adequate funding, competent professionals, and skilled laborers for the construction. Please give us favor with the surrounding communities and the nation. Father, stir up the faith in me so that I will walk by faith and not by sight and give to this vision.

Father, please forgive us for questioning the vision You have given to our Pastor and for not submitting to his/her authority. Forgive us for having loose lips and speaking idle words against this project. Forgive us Lord for not coming together as a church body concerning the building project. Please forgive us for all of our sins. Father, remind us of those we need to forgive and we will be quick to forgive.

As a Church Family, please do not lead us to temptation; but deliver us from evil.

Yours, O Lord, is the greatness, the power, the glory, the victory, and the majesty. Everything in the heavens and on earth is Yours, and this is Your Kingdom. We adore You as the One who is over all things. In Jesus' name, amen.

Scripture References for the Written Text

Lamentations 3:22-23, Isaiah 45:18-19, Zechariah 2:5, Matthew 6:10, Proverbs 16:3, Proverbs 15:22, Habakkuk 2:2, Exodus 31:1-6,

Philippians 1:6, 1 Thessalonians 5:17, 2 Corinthians 5:7, Matthew 6:13, 1 Chronicles 29:11

Today, I will trust God to:

_____

_____

_____

_____

_____

_____

_____

_____

_____

Prayer Petition 4: A Prayer for Our Families

Scripture Reading: Psalm 145:1-13, Psalm 128

Reflections of the Heart

It is the Lord's good pleasure to bless our families. So, *"may the Lord, the God of our ancestors, multiply our families a thousand times more and bless us as He has promised"* (Deut. 1:11 NLT).

Scriptural Prayer:

Heavenly Father, our souls honor You. Your power is absolute. Your understanding is beyond comprehension. We love and exalt You our God and King. You have taught children and infants to tell of Your strength. What are mere mortals that You should think about them, human beings that You should care for them? We know Your greatness, Lord; You are greater than any other god. You do whatever pleases You throughout all Heaven and earth and on the seas and in their depths. Father, we thank You for our family relationships. We thank You for the institution of marriage and parenthood. Lord, we thank You for fulfilling Your plans and purposes in our lives and for surrounding us with favor like a shield. Thank You for continually blessing us with Your loving-kindness and tender mercies. Your faithful love endures forever.

Father, it is Your will that men and women marry and create new families. It is Your will that our families prosper and be in health as our souls prosper. We declare that our families live in safety, quietly at home where we find rest. We declare that stability, salvation, love, wisdom, and knowledge abide in our homes. We confess that our husbands love their wives as Christ loved the Church and that our wives respect their husbands. We confess that the husbands of this church body are blameless, faithful to their wives, wise, and just. We declare that they live devout and disciplined lives. They are not arrogant or quick-tempered; they are not heavy drinkers, violent or dishonest with money. We confess that they rule their own houses well. We declare that our children are obedient, for this is right in Your sight. Lord, as a church family, we come against bickering, slander, strife, the spirits of perversion, violence, offense, lies, rebellion, disobedience, and cruelty in our families. We break all soul ties, strongholds, and generational curses in our bloodlines. We confess that no weapon formed against our families will prosper. We confess that everything that the devil means for evil will be turned around by our God for our good. We call for a spiritual revival in our families. Father, we will hold tightly, without wavering, to the hope we affirm; for we know that You can be trusted to keep Your promise. We confess that the love of God will reign supreme in our homes and that the peace of God is an umpire in our family relationships.

Father, we ask that You would give each of our families a single-ness of heart and put a new spirit within them. Where there are strained relationships in our families, please turn hearts back to one another. Give us Your wisdom. Let discretion preserve us and understanding keep us from the way of evil. Please unite our families closer together. Holy Spirit, empower married couples to be the priests, prophets, husbands, wives, fathers, mothers, pro-viders, protectors and leaders of their homes. Help them not to provoke their children to anger, but to bring them up in the training and admonition of the Lord. Help our single parents to be the priests, prophets, parents, nurturers, providers, protectors, and leaders of their homes. Lord, strengthen and impart Your wisdom into the lives of our single parents. Help them to model a life that is pleasing to You. Holy Spirit, please help our singles to live with all godliness and contentment, which is great gain. For those singles who desire a mate, help them to wait patiently on You. Father, open the lines of communication in our homes so that there is a good rapport in our families. Please keep our chil-dren and youth as the apple of Your eye, and let Your favor sur-round them like a shield. Let peace, love, and understanding reside in our families.

Father, please forgive our families for sin. Forgive all of us for acts of sinfulness, including bitterness, resentment, adultery, fornica-tion, spousal abuse, child abuse, envy, strife, unkindness, rebel-lion, deception, doubt, fear, injustice, economic mismanagement, poor parenting, and oppression. Lord, remind us to forgive one another, as well as others, and help us to forgive.

Lead us not into temptation; but deliver us from the evil one.

Praise the Lord! Salvation and glory and power belong to You. Your judgments are true and just. You, the Lord God Almighty, reign. Who will not fear You, Lord, and glorify Your name? You alone are holy. All nations will come and worship before You for Your righteous deeds have been revealed. You are our eternal king. In Jesus' name, amen.

Scripture References for the Written Text

Psalm 147:5, Psalm 145:1, Psalm 8:2, 4, Psalm 135:5-6, Psalm 5:12, Psalm 136:1, Genesis 1:27-28, 3 John 2, Isaiah 32:18, Ephesians 5:25, 22, Titus 1:6-8, Ephesians 6:1, Isaiah 54:17, Genesis 50:20, Hebrews 10:23, Ezekiel 11:19, Proverbs 2:11, Ephesians 6:4, 1 Timothy 6:6, Psalm 17:8, Psalm 5:12, Matthew 6:13, Revelation 19:1-2,6, Revelation 15:4

Today, I will trust God to:

_____

_____

_____

_____

_____

_____

_____

_____

_____

_____

Prayer Petition 5: A Prayer for Men

Scripture Reading: Exodus 15:2-18, 2 Kings 18:1-7

Reflections of the Heart

God loves men and He wired them for success. The enemy has been disrupting God's preferred plans for our men through a strategy to steal, kill, and destroy them. Archbishop Nicholas Duncan Williams noted, "Life is not fair; we only get what we are willing to fight for!" By praying for our men, boys, and families, we are positioned to "Fight to Win!" God used a man to redeem humankind, and He continues to empower men to lead and conquer.

Scriptural Prayer:

Heavenly Father, Your majestic name fills the earth! Your glory is higher than the heavens. May Your glorious name be praised! May it be exalted above all blessing and praise! You are great and most worthy of praise! No one can measure Your greatness. Thank You, Father, for our men. Lord, we thank You for equipping our men to take their rightful place in You. Thank You for the men and boys who will join the Body of Christ and glorify Your name. Thank You, God, for restoration, reconciliation, and healing in our families and communities. Thank You, for giving us everything that we need to live a godly life.

Father, let Your Kingdom come and Your will be done in the lives of our men on earth as it is in Heaven. By faith, we call our men saved, sanctified, and filled with Your Spirit. Your Word instructs that faith without works is dead and useless, so we confess that our men will work to develop and demonstrate their Christian faith, daily. We declare that they will be priestly providers and protectors of their families. We confess that, as they submit to Your Word, they will be transformed into new people by changing the way they think. Lord, we decree that their belief systems and behavior patterns will reflect Your righteousness in their personal and professional lives. We declare that the light of Jesus will be reflected by their actions. As they fellowship with one another, others will see their good works and praise You, our Father in Heaven. Lord, we confess that Your favor surrounds them like a shield. We confess that they will earn, save, spend, and invest money in obedience to Your perfect plan for their lives and families. We declare that their finances are blessed and that they are lenders, not borrowers. Lord, because we realize that the food we put in our bodies can impact our mental, emotional, physical, and spiritual capabilities, we declare that our men will practice healthy eating practices. Above all, we confess that they are victorious in everything they do because Your future for them is filled with hope and good, not evil.

Lord, we ask that You touch the hearts of our congregation to pray for the men and boys of this local assembly. Holy Spirit, please empower us all to stand against society's systems and structures that result in many pre-school boys being suspended. Holy Spirit, studies show that a very high percent of all "behavioral problems" in public schools are linked to boys. Please touch the hearts of fathers (and mothers) to teach their children Your godly principles.

Father, forgive our men for the sins of disobedience, selfishness, lying, pornography, fornication, and adultery and for rejecting the responsibility for leadership within their families and the Church. Forgive our boys for rebellion and selfishness and for accepting the negative labels placed on them by the world. Forgive our wives and mothers for being complacent. Lord, please help the men, women, boys, and girls in our congregation to forgive past hurts caused by family members and loved ones. Father, heal emotional wounds caused by these hurts. Lord, remind all of us to forgive others and help us to forgive.

Lead us not into temptation; but deliver us from the evil one.

Lord, we praise Your Name. Your Name is very great; Your glory towers over the earth and heaven. You are worthy, Lord, to receive glory, honor and power. You created all things, and they exist because You created what You pleased. You are Wonderful,

Counselor, Mighty God, Everlasting Father, and Prince of Peace. In Jesus' name, amen.

Scripture References for the Written Text

Psalm 8:1, Nehemiah 9:5, Psalm 145:3, 2 Peter 1:3, Matthew 6:10, Hebrews 11:1, James 2:17, Romans 12:2, Matthew 5:16, Psalm 5:12, Deuteronomy 28:12, Jeremiah 29:11, Matthew 6:13, Psalm 148:13, Revelation 4:11, Isaiah 9:6

Today, I will trust God to:

_____

_____

_____

_____

_____

_____

_____

_____

Prayer Petition 6: A Prayer for Women

Scripture Reading: Psalm 97, Colossians 1:9-14

Reflections of the Heart

Women are God's woven tapestry. God loves women so much that He sent His Son to earth through one. Created in His image, women are the strength and beauty of a society; whether single or married, may our lives be a daily reflection of His Glory!

Scriptural Prayer

Heavenly Father, You are our God and there is none other. We worship You in the splendor of Your Holiness. You are the true and living God to whom all honor and glory belongs. We thank You for creating us in Your image. We earnestly search for You; our souls thirst for You, and our bodies long for You in this land where there is no water. Thank You for having good plans for our lives, to give us a future and a hope, and not plans for disaster. We declare our thanks and devotion to You for Your goodness and loving-kindness toward us. We will love You, Lord, our strength. You are our Rock, our fortress, and our Savior. You are our God, our strength in whom we will trust. Thank You, Father, for blessing the women of our church and community.

Lord, You created women to be the mothers of humanity. Today, we declare that the women of our church will not copy the behavior and customs of this world, but they will be transformed by the Holy Spirit to do what is good and pleasing and perfect in Your sight. We confess that our women will possess love, joy, peace, long-suffering, kindness, goodness, faithfulness, gentleness, and self-control. We declare that our wives will honor their husbands and submit themselves to God by loving their husbands. We confess that our single women will excel in their academic and professional careers and that they will devote themselves to serving God. Our women are blessed, and they shall flourish like palm trees and be as strong as the cedars of Lebanon. They are planted in the house of our God, and they shall flourish in His courts. Our women will bear fruit in their old age and they shall be fresh and flourishing. They will declare that the Lord is just, that He is their Rock, and that there is no evil in Him. We declare that our mothers will direct their children onto the right path, and their children, when they are older, will not leave that path. We confess with holy boldness that our women, who are mothers, will give their children the Word of God, love, and encouragement.

Father, we ask You to give each woman a complete knowledge of Your will along with spiritual wisdom and understanding. Please order their days so that their daily activities are balanced and fruitful. Make the crooked places in our families straight and perfect those things that concern them. Please help our singles and married women to live with all godliness and contentment, which is great gain. For those singles who desire a mate, help them to wait patiently on You. Knit the hearts of our married women closer together with their husbands and give them courage to live Your Word in every facet of their marriage. Father, please restore the broken places in those marriages that are struggling. Increase Your love and security in those marriages that are doing well. Father, we ask You to bless all the women of our church family.

Father, please forgive our women for not trusting You with their lives. Forgive them for quick tempers and lack of patience. Forgive those who are mothers for not raising their children according to Your Word. Forgive mothers for allowing the television, radio, video games, music, older siblings, and activities to raise their children. Forgive mothers for saying negative words against their children's fathers. Forgive both married and single women for not seeking help when feeling anxious, depressed, fretful, angry, and overwhelmed. Father, please forgive our women for all of their sins. Lord, remind us all to forgive, and help us to be quick to forgive.

Lead us not into temptation; but deliver us from the evil one.

Father, You laid the foundations of the earth and determined its dimensions. You keep the sea inside its boundaries and declared that the proud waves must stop and go no farther. You command the morning to appear and cause the dawn to rise in the east. You make daylight spread to the ends of the earth and bring an end to the night's wickedness. The Lord of Heaven's Armies is Your name! In Jesus' name, amen.

Scripture References for the Written Text

Psalm 29:2, Genesis 1:26, Psalm 63:1, Jeremiah 29:11, Psalm 18:1-2, Genesis 3:20, Romans 12:2, Galatians 5:22-23, Ephesians 5:22, 1 Corinthians 7:32, Psalm 92:12-15, Proverbs 22:6, Colossians 1:9, Isaiah 42:16, 1 Timothy 6:6, Matthew 6:13, Job 38:4-5,8,11-13

Today, I will trust God to:

_____

_____

_____

_____

_____

_____

_____

_____

_____

Prayer Petition 7: A Prayer for Children

Scripture Reading: Psalm 95:1-7, Daniel 1:8-21

Reflections of the Heart

We declare that our children are heirs of righteousness! Each day they are growing in wisdom and stature. They have favor both with God and men.

Scriptural Prayer

Our Father in Heaven, we shout joyfully to You, the Rock of our salvation. We come to You with thanksgiving for You are the great God and the great King above all gods. You hold the depths of the earth and the mightiest mountains in Your hands. The sea belongs to You for You made it. Your hands formed the dry land too. We come to worship and bow down; we kneel before You, our Lord and Maker. You are our God, and we are the people You watch over, the flock under Your care. We thank You for life, health, and strength. Thank You for blessing us with strong, healthy, and vibrant children. Thank You for [specifically call out each child's name].

Father, it is Your will that, as parents, we walk in integrity so that our children are blessed. It is Your will that our children are taught of You and Your Word so that they will enjoy great peace. It is Your will that they hide Your Word in their hearts that they might not sin against You. It is Your will that our children be bold and courageous in their obedience to You. We confess that Your will for our children is for Your Word to be fully operative in their lives. We realize that obedience to Your Word gives our children wisdom, and living daily according to the guidance of the Holy Spirit gives them power. We confess that our children obey Your Word. We declare that they walk by faith and not by sight. In Jesus' name, they will trust You with all of their hearts and not depend on their own understanding. We declare that You will be the center of everything they do, and we expect their paths to be straight.

Holy Spirit, we ask You to touch the hearts of our children to confess with their mouths the Lord Jesus and to believe in their hearts that God raised Jesus from the dead so that they are saved. Please circumcise their hearts to love You, the Lord their God, with all their hearts and souls. Holy Spirit, please lead and guide them to Your truth. We pray that You would help our children to keep the statutes, judgments, and commandments of God so that they might have wisdom and understanding. Teach them how to activate the power of God as they walk according to You, Holy Spirit, and not their flesh. Let the mind of Christ be in them so that they will act, talk, and think like Jesus. Remind them to not put other gods before our Heavenly Father. Help them to honor and obey their parents so that they will live long, full lives and so that things may go well with them.

Father, please forgive parents for any abuse or neglect. Forgive parents for being so preoccupied with their own needs that they fail to have structure in their homes for healthy meals, support for educational needs, and training for good manners and citizenship. Forgive parents for being selfish, self-centered, and single-minded. Lord, remind us all of those we need to forgive; and help us to be quick to forgive.

Lead us not to temptation; but deliver us from the evil one.

Lord, You are the Lion of the tribe of Judah, the heir to David's throne, the victorious One. Your Name is above all other names. At the name of Jesus, every knee should bow in Heaven and on earth and under the earth. Every tongue will confess that You, Jesus Christ, are Lord, to the glory of God the Father. In Jesus' name, amen.

Scripture References for the Written Text

Psalm 95:1-7, Proverbs 20:7, Isaiah 54:13, Psalm 119:11, Joshua 1:8, 2 Corinthians 5:7, Proverbs 3:5, Isaiah 42:16, Romans 10:9, Deuteronomy 30:6, Deuteronomy 4:6, Galatians 5:16, Philippians 2:5, Exodus 20:3, Ephesians 6:1-3, Matthew 6:13, Revelation 5:5, Philippians 2:9-11

Today, I will trust God to:

_____

_____

_____

_____

_____

_____

_____

_____

Prayer Petition 8: A Prayer for Healthy Pregnancies and Healthy Babies

Scripture Reading: Psalm 135:1-7, Psalm 127:3-5

Reflections of the Heart

Very few things bring as much excitement as a new baby. Every baby and child is a gift from God. As a matter of fact, each is a reward from the Lord—one of God's miracles of life. Pray for those in our church family who are expecting their miracle soon and for those whose miracle has arrived.

Scriptural Prayer

Sovereign Lord, You are great! There is no one like You. We have never even heard of another God like You! Your throne endures forever and ever. You rule with a scepter of justice. You love justice and hate evil. You are our God, and we earnestly search for You. Our souls thirst for You; we long for You in our bodies in this parched and weary land where there is no water. We have seen

You in Your sanctuary and gazed upon Your power and glory. Your unfailing love is better than life itself; how we praise You! Father, we thank You for being the source of life. Thank You for every expectant mother in our congregation. Thank You for every child that has been born into our church family.

Father, we declare that the children who are born into this church family are healthy and well-loved. Lord, You knit them together in their mother's womb. We declare that each baby is wonderfully made. Your workmanship is marvelous! You made all of their delicate, inner parts. Today, we confess that every baby in utero has exactly 46 chromosomes and that they will develop without defect or deformity. We declare that every anatomical system, cell, muscle, tissue, and organ will develop according to Your divine purpose and plan. We decree that mothers will carry their babies to full term. We destroy every demonic assignment against our unborn, including the assignment of premature birth. In Jesus' name, there will be no miscarriages or infertility in our congregation. We proclaim that sickness and disease, including SIDS, autism, Down Syndrome, ADD, ADHD, juvenile diabetes, cancer, dyslexia, and all other childhood diseases or dysfunctions have no legal right to inhabit our children because God is their Shepherd and Shield. As a church family, we cry out for our children who have been diagnosed with a disease or disorder. In Jesus' name, we command God's divine healing to manifest in their bodies, from the crowns of their heads to the soles of their feet, now! We decree that, by Jesus' stripes, they are healed. We proclaim that our children will grow and develop into mighty men and women of God. We confess that our children can learn and process information properly. They will do all things through Christ who strengthens them, including excelling academically.

Father, we ask You to increase Your wisdom and knowledge in every expectant mother. Holy Spirit, remind them to get the proper rest and nutrition. Lord, watch over each expectant mother and keep her body healthy. Provide a support network of family and friends who will help them during and after their pregnancies. Strengthen the minds, bodies, and spirits of parents who have children with special needs. Holy Spirit, show us, as a church family, how we can support and help them. Cause Your peace to be still in the minds, hearts, and spirits of those mothers who are fearful and anxious. Please provide financial miracles for families who are struggling financially. Father, there is nothing too difficult for You.

Father, please forgive our parents and expectant parents for any acts of sinfulness. Forgive those who have committed fornication or adultery. Forgive parents for stubbornness, quick tempers, and lack of patience. Forgive them for not seeking help when they are feeling anxious, depressed, fretful, angry, or overwhelmed. Forgive us as a church family for not offering more support to our parents. Forgive us for the times when we have been insensitive to those families who have children with special needs. Lord, remind all of us of those we need to forgive, and help us to be quick to forgive.

Lead our parents not into temptation; but deliver them from the evil one.

God, You are greater than we can understand. Your years cannot be counted. You draw up the water vapor and distill it into rain. Only You know where light comes from and where darkness goes. You direct the movement of the stars, binding the cluster of the Pleiades and loosening the cords of Orion. Holy and triumphant is Your Name! In Jesus' name, amen.

Scripture References for the Written Text

2 Samuel 7:22, Psalm 45:6-7, Psalm 63:1-3, Psalm 139:13-14, Matthew 11:23, Mark 11:23, Job 22:28, Philippians 4:13, Psalm 34:17, Isaiah 53:5, Matthew 6:13, Job 36:26-27, Job 38:19,31

Today, I will trust God to:

_____

_____

_____

_____

_____

_____

_____

_____

Prayer Petition 9: A Prayer for Finances

Scripture Reading: Jeremiah 10:6-16, Malachi 3:1-8

Reflections of the Heart

"Let those who favor my righteous cause and have pleasure in my uprightness shout for joy and be glad and say continually, let the Lord be magnified, who takes pleasure in the prosperity of His servant" (Ps. 35:27).

Scriptural Prayer

Father, You are great, and You perform wonderful deeds. You alone are God. Lord, You are in Your Holy temple; You rule from Heaven. To You, O God, do we give thanks. Yes, to You do we give thanks. We thank You for Your eternal love and unmerited grace. We thank You for Your unfailing love for us that never ends and

Your mercies which never cease. Your mercies are new every morning; great is Your faithfulness. We exalt You, our God and King, and we praise Your name forever and ever. Thank You, Father, for being our strength, our shield, our provider, and our Savior. Thank You for blessing us with jobs that provide us with income. Thank You for promotions and raises. Thank You for favor with our bosses and co-workers.

Father, we confess that we will save, spend, and invest money in obedience to Your perfect plan for our lives and our families. We confess that, as You bring financial blessings into our lives, we will remember that You give us the power to get wealth. We declare that we are set on high above the nations of the earth because we diligently obey Your voice and carefully observe Your commandments. Father, we confess that all that we set our hands to do is blessed because You have commanded blessings on our storehouses, including savings, investments, and retirement accounts. Lord, we declare that, as Your blessings overtake us, we will be able to lend money to many and not have to borrow from anyone. We confess that, as we bring the tithes into Your house, we expect You to pour out blessings so large that we will not have room to receive them. Lord, we declare that we will be faithful stewards of Your financial blessings, and we expect You to confirm Your Word and make us rulers over abundant wealth. We call forth a new anointing of entrepreneurship, new ideas, and new businesses in our communities. Lord, we call forth a spirit of excellence and prosperity in our finances and in all areas of our lives.

Holy Spirit, please shift our focus from spending to saving and from consuming our income to building wealth. We ask You to help us tie loyalty and kindness around our necks and write them deep within our hearts so that we may find favor with both You and people and earn a good reputation. Father, we pray for promotions and financial increase. Holy Spirit, help us to study the

Word, to meditate on it day and night, and to observe to do the things written within it so that we may make our way prosperous and have success in all that we do. Help us to build business and personal relationships with other Christians, and give us favor with the business community. Help us to begin to love people and use money, rather than loving money and using people. We pray for a breaking of old mindsets and generational curses of poverty and lack within our families.

Father, forgive us for our sins. Forgive us for repeating patterns of financial failures such as living beyond our means and misusing credit cards. Forgive us for failing to develop financial plans that include debt reduction, savings, and investments. Forgive many of us for believing that we are supposed to have the most of the worst and the least of the best. Forgive us for not recognizing that You will not withhold any good thing from us, as we walk uprightly before You. Forgive us for words and thoughts of doubt and unbelief. Father, forgive us for walking by sight, rather than walking by faith. Lord, remind us of those we need to forgive, and we will be quick to forgive.

Lead us not into temptation; but deliver us from the evil one.

Lord, You are our Savior. You are the hope of everyone on earth. You formed the mountains by Your power and armed Yourself with mighty strength. You quieted the raging oceans with their pounding waves and silenced the shouting of the nations. Those who live at the ends of the earth stand in awe of Your wonders. From where the sun rises to where it sets, You inspire shouts of joy. In Jesus' name, amen.

Scripture References for the Written Text

Psalm 86:10, Psalm 11:4, Lamentations 3:22-23, Psalm 145:1, Deuteronomy 8:18, Deuteronomy 28:1-2, 8, 12, Malachi 3:10,

Matthew 25:21, Proverbs 3:3-4, Joshua 1:8, Psalm 84:11, 2 Corinthians 5:7, Matthew 6: 13, Psalm 65:5-8

Today, I will trust God to:

_____

_____

_____

_____

_____

_____

_____

_____

_____

Prayer Petition 10: A Prayer for Forgiveness and Forgiving Others

Scripture Reading: Nehemiah 9:6-15, Matthew 6:9-15

Reflections of the Heart

When we ask God to forgive us, what do we really expect? He said He would cast our sins into the sea of forgetfulness and never remember them. Do we believe this? Today, trust the Lord to purge you with His hyssop and wash you whiter than snow. He said He would forgive us. As you admit any wrongdoing, confess them with the confidence of knowing that God loves you and that He wants what is best for you.

Scriptural Prayer

Father, we honor You and we bless You. With all our souls and all that is within us, we bless Your holy Name. It is You, Father, who crowns us with love and tender mercies, and You fill our lives with good things. We give thanks to You and proclaim Your greatness. Lord, we will let the whole world know what You have done. We will sing to You the praises due Your Name and tell everyone about Your wonderful deeds. Thank You, Father, for loving us, forgiving us, and saving us. Thank You for being patient with us. Your compassion toward us is unfailing, and Your mercies are new every morning. Lord, Your faithfulness is great toward us.

Father, Your Word tells us that if we forgive those who have sinned against us, then You, our Heavenly Father, will forgive us. But, if we refuse to forgive others, You will not forgive us of our sins. Today we choose to forgive. Father, we declare that we will be patient with people and forgive those who have offended us. I forgive [name the persons you need to forgive] for [say specifically what you are forgiving them for], and I release them and let it go. Father, forgive me for my sins. You said that if I confess my sins to You, You are faithful and just to forgive me and cleanse me from all wickedness. Therefore, Father, please forgive me for [say specifically what you want the Lord to forgive you for].

Holy Spirit, help all of us to forgive people who have hurt us. Heal our emotions that have been wounded, and teach us how to love unconditionally. Continue to extend Your love and mercy toward us. Please remind us daily to use Your power that lives on the inside of us which helps us in all things. Lord, help us to forget the past so that we can move forward to the future as we press toward the mark of our higher calling in Christ Jesus.

Father, please forgive us for not being forgiving. Forgive us for thinking evil thoughts and seeking revenge against people who have offended us. Forgive us for hatred and for not walking in love. Forgive us for gossiping, lying, and rehearsing in our minds what was said or done to us. Lord, remind us of those persons we need to forgive, and help us to forgive.

Lead us not into temptation; but deliver us from the evil one.

God, You are a mighty fortress. You are subject to none, yet, all are subject to You. You are the Alpha and Omega, the beginning and the end. You are the God who is, and was, and who is to come. To You, the King eternal, immortal, invisible, the only wise God, be honor and glory forever and ever. Yours is the Kingdom and the power and the glory forever. In Jesus' name, amen.

Scripture References for the written text

Psalm 103:1-5, 1 Chronicles 16:8-9, Lamentations 3:22-23, Matthew 6:14-15, Ephesians 4:2, 1 John 1:9, Philippians 3:14, Matthew 6:13, Revelation 1:8, 1 Timothy 1:17

Today, I will trust God to:

_____

_____

_____

_____

_____

_____

_____

_____

Prayer Petition 11: A Prayer for Physical Healing

Scripture Reading: Psalm 111, James 5:13-16

Reflections of the Heart

Divine healing is as real today as it was in the book of Acts. Jesus is the same today, yesterday, and forever! In Mark 16:17-18, Jesus said, *"These signs will accompany those who believe: They will cast out demons in my name, and they will speak new languages. They will be able to handle snakes with safety, and if they drink anything poisonous, it won't hurt them. They will be able to place their hands on the sick and heal them."* Let us do what Jesus did!

Scriptural Prayer

Father, You are great, and You perform wonderful deeds. You alone are God. How great are Your signs and how powerful are Your wonders. Lord, You are high above all the nations. Your glory is higher than the heavens. Who can be compared with You, our God, who is enthroned on high? We give thanks because You are near. People everywhere will tell of Your wonderful deeds. Lord, we thank You for salvation, the greatest miracle of all. Thank You for Your eternal love and unmerited grace. Thank You for sending Your Son, Jesus, to break the power of the devil and to bring us hope, health, and healing. Lord, You are good and Your unfailing love endures forever.

Lord, You brought Israel out of Egypt with signs and wonders, with a strong hand and powerful arm. Jesus Christ, Your Son, turned water into wine, cleansed lepers, healed the sick, raised the dead, and fed 5000 people with two fish and five loaves of bread. Jesus did many other signs in the presence of His disciples so that we would believe that He is the Christ, the Son of God, and have life in His name. We believe Jesus Christ is the same, yesterday, today, and forever. Therefore, Father we expect You to display Your glory in the lives of those persons who are in need of healing and deliverance. With You, nothing is impossible. We expect diseases to be dissolved, broken relationships to be mended, and those who are held captive in their minds and souls to be set free. As we pray for those in need of healing, we confess that Your healing power will operate through us.

Father, please help us to be bolder about praying for healing. Help those in need of healing to trust in You with all of their hearts and not to depend on their own understanding. Holy Spirit, please open the eyes of their understanding so that they will understand the confident hope You have given to those You have called in the miraculous. Remind people to look to You for help, strength, and power. Father, cause Your healing to be experienced throughout our church and community.

Father, forgive those persons who have doubted Your Word and Your works. Forgive them for acting religious, but rejecting the power that could make them godly and denying Your power to perform healings, signs, and wonders in their lives and in the lives of others. Lord, please forgive them and restore to them the joy of Your salvation. Lord, remind people of those they need to forgive, and help them to be quick to forgive.

Lead those in need of healing not into temptation; but deliver them from the evil one.

Father, You are the Almighty! Only You can open the eyes of the blind and unplug the ears of the deaf. You cause the lame to leap like deer and those who cannot speak to sing for joy. You cause springs to gush forth in the wilderness and streams to water the wasteland. You cause the parched ground to become a pool and springs of water to satisfy the thirsty land. Great and awesome is Your Name. In Jesus' name, amen.

Scripture References for the written text

Psalm 86:10, Daniel 4:3, Psalm 113:4-5, Psalm 75:1, Psalm 136:1, Psalm 136:11-12, John 2:1-9, Luke 7:22, Matthew 14:14-21, John 20:30-31, Hebrews 13:8, Luke 1:37, Proverbs 3:5, Ephesians 1:18, 2 Timothy 3:5, Matthew 6:13, Isaiah 35:5-7

Today, I will trust God to:

_____

_____

_____

_____

_____

_____

_____

_____

Prayer Petition 12: A Prayer for Mental Healing

Scripture Reading: Psalm 18:1-31, Psalm 42

Reflections of the Heart

We receive comfort in these words, *"Those who wait on the Lord will find new strength. They will fly high on wings like eagles. They will run and not grow weary. They will walk and not faint"* (Isa. 40:31 NLT).

Scriptural Prayer

Father, You are great and most worthy of praise. You are to be feared above all gods. The earth is Yours and everything in it; the world and all its people belong to You. You laid the earth's foundation on the seas and built it on the ocean's depths. You are the King of glory, the Lord strong and mighty. You are the Lord, invincible in battle. O Lord, you have performed many wonders for us. Your plans for us are too numerous to list. You have no equal. We are grateful that when we, Your people, call to You for help, You hear and rescue us out of our troubles. Thank You for giving us Your peace and joy. Thank You for providing a life of hope, abundance, and destiny. Thank You for being our strength in times of weakness.

Father, You said that You would give rest to all who are weary and heavy burdened. Your yoke is easy, and Your burdens are light. We are supposed to trust in You with all of our hearts and not depend on our own understanding. We are to seek Your will in all that we do, and You will show us which path to take. You are the God who will bring rest to our souls. We trust in Your Word and believe that Your Word will be operative in the hearts and souls of those with mental illnesses. We confess that, when they walk in the midst of trouble, You will revive them and stretch forth Your hand and save them. You have left Your gift of peace of mind with them, and we pray that their hearts will not be afraid. We confess, even though they may be pressed on every side by troubles, that they will not be crushed and broken. They may feel perplexed, but they will not give up and quit. They may be hunted down, but You will never abandon them. They may be knocked down, but they will get up and keep going. Father, we confess that they will lie down without fear and enjoy pleasant dreams. They will not be afraid of the threat of disaster or destruction; You are their security.

Holy Spirit, we ask You to replace sadness with joy, defeat with victory, and fatigue with praise. Help those who feel depressed or sad to not focus on their circumstances, but rather focus on Your blessings in their lives. Remind them to praise You at all times. We ask that You bring all things to their memory that concern You and Your plans for their lives. Give them power as they meditate on Your Word. Help them to keep Your commandments and embrace them in their hearts. Father, help them to not be conformed to this world, but transformed by the renewing of their minds. Holy Spirit, we ask that You strengthen and renew their innermost being. Let the fiery darts of the enemy not permeate their being. May they always hear Your voice and obey Your will. Father, please help them to overcome their fears. Please strengthen their family members and caretakers and help them to always walk in Your peace and love with their loved one(s).

Father, forgive them for sin. Forgive them for worry and fear. Forgive them for being anxious. Forgive them for not being diligent in fasting and praying. Forgive them for not trusting You at all times. Lord, remind them of those they need to forgive; and help them be quick to forgive.

Lead them not into temptation; but deliver them from the evil one.

Father, You are the Lord God Almighty! Let the whole world glorify You, Lord; let it sing Your praises! You will march forth like a mighty hero. You will come out like a warrior, full of fury. You will shout Your battle cry and crush all of Your enemies. You alone are worthy to receive glory and honor and power. In Jesus' name, Amen.

Scripture References for the Written Text

Psalm 96:4, Psalm 24:1-2,8, Psalm 40:5, Psalm 34:17, Matthew 11:28, Proverbs 3:5-6, Psalm 138:7, John 14:27, 2 Corinthians 4:8-9, Proverbs 3:24, Psalm 91:6, Psalm 34:1, John 14:26, Romans 12:2, Matthew 6:13, Isaiah 42:12-13, Revelation 4:11

Today, I will trust God to:

_____

_____

_____

_____

_____

_____

_____

_____

_____

Prayer Petition 13: Prayer for Business Leaders

Scripture Reading: Psalm 95, Deuteronomy 8

Reflections of the Heart

Godly business leaders should be mindful of the seven things the Lord detests: haughty eyes, lying tongues, hands that kill the innocent, hearts that plot evil, feet that race to do wrong, false witnesses who pour out lies, and persons who sow discord among brothers. God needs business leaders who will incorporate His principles in their business practices. As our business leaders walk in godly integrity, their businesses will grow and our communities will reap the benefits.

Scriptural Prayer

Father, to You we sing a new song. Your praises will be sung from the ends of the earth. Your praises will be shouted from the mountaintops! Let the whole world glorify You, Lord. We bless You because You are the Lord, our God, the Holy One of Israel, our Savior. Lord, You always keep Your promises, and You are gracious in all that You do. You help those who have fallen and lift those who are bent beneath their loads. Thank You for blessing the business community in our city throughout the years. Thank You, Father, for opening doors of opportunity that have produced profit *and employment. Thank You for increasing economic development in our city.*

Father, we declare that Your Word will be operative in the lives of our business leaders and in the economic development of our city. Father, we declare that our business leaders are blessed, and we expect favor to surround them like a shield. We confess that, as our leaders commit their works to You, their plans will be established. We declare that they will honor You with their possessions and with the first fruits of all their increase so that their barns will be filled and their vats will overflow with new wine. We declare that whatever they do, they will do it heartily, as to You and not to men. Lord, we confess that as our business leaders walk uprightly, no good thing will be withheld from them. Father, we expect You to look favorably upon the economic development in our city and bless our city to be fruitful.

Father, we ask that Your Spirit of wisdom, understanding, counsel, and power would rest on each business leader, investor, and entrepreneur. Fill them with the knowledge of Your will and give them a thirst for Your Word so that they can incorporate Your principles into their business practices. Help them to make righteous decisions and operate with justice and integrity. Give them dreams and visions that exceed their expectations and provide them with the resources they need to successfully accomplish Your purpose(s) for their businesses. Father, encourage potential business leaders and entrepreneurs to write down Your vision for their businesses and make it plain in a business plan so that they and their investors can implement it. We ask You to reveal new revenue streams within the business community. Lord, please continue to bless the marketplace in our city so that it will reflect Your glory and benefit the people living in it. Lord, show me what I can do to help improve the economy of our city.

Father, forgive our business leaders for all acts of sinfulness. Forgive those who have not been diligent in seeking Your leadership for their business. Forgive those who do not trust in You but lean to their own understanding. Forgive those who have compromised Your Word in order to make a profit. Forgive those who have not treated their employees and customers fairly. Forgive those who have not been faithful in giving through tithes and offerings. Forgive those who have not properly taken care of or shown respect for the community they live in. Forgive me for not supporting those businesses You have established in my community. Remind the entrepreneurs and business owners in our city to be forgiving; and help them to forgive.

Lead them not into temptation; but deliver them from the evil one.

Lord, You sit above the circle of the earth. The people below seem like grasshoppers to You. You spread out the heavens like a curtain and made Your tents from them. You judge the great people of the world and bring them all to nothing. You are the I AM that I AM. In Jesus' name, amen.

Scripture References for the written text

Isaiah 42:10-13, Isaiah 43:3, Psalm 145:13-14, Psalm 5:12, Proverbs 16:3, Proverbs 3:9-10, Colossians 3:23, Psalm 84:11, Leviticus 26:9, Colossians 1:9-12, Habakkuk 2:2, Matthew 6:13, Isaiah 40:22-23, Exodus 3:14

Today, I will trust God to:

_____

_____

_____

_____

_____

_____

_____

_____

Prayer Petition 14: A Prayer for Elections in the United States

Scripture Reading: Psalm 148, 1 Samuel 16:1-13

Reflections of the Heart

In the Bible, God was directly involved in the selection of kings, priests, and judges. It was important to Him to have men and women who would lead His people in righteousness, justice, and holiness. Today, God is just as concerned about who leads the nations of this world. When you pray, seek His wisdom about the presidential candidates, and then exercise your right to vote under His direction.

Scriptural Prayer

Our Father, we praise Your Name forever and ever, for You possess all wisdom and power. You control the course of world events. You remove kings and set up other kings. You give wisdom to the wise and knowledge to the scholars. You reveal deep and mysterious things and know what lays hidden in darkness, though You are surrounded by light. Father, we thank You for the United States of America. As citizens of this nation, we thank You for the opportunity to have a voice in the selection of our leaders. Jesus, we thank You for continuing to bless our nation. Holy Spirit, thank You for Your guidance and power. You are an awesome God.

Heavenly Father, let Your Kingdom come and Your will be done during the election process. Your Word states that we are to pray for kings and all people who are in authority so that we can live peaceful and quiet lives that are marked by godliness and dignity. We know that this is good and acceptable in Your sight. In obedience to Your Word, we intercede for the U.S. election process. We lift up all elected officials before You, along with their entire staff and volunteers. As the election process comes to an end, we confess that each candidate will not walk in the counsel of the ungodly, nor stand in the paths of sinners, nor sit in the seat of the scornful, but that their delight will be in Your law and they will meditate on Your Word day and night. We confess that they are like trees planted by the rivers of water who will bring forth fruit in their season. Their leaves will not wither, and whatever they do will prosper for the good of the nation.

Father, You are a God of order; therefore we command Your order to operate within each candidate's campaign now! We decree that no weapon formed against them will prosper and that every tongue, which rises against them in judgment, will be condemned by God. Peace, be still! We decree that every attempt to misconstrue the Truth will be confused, in Jesus' name. We declare that the democratic process will be implemented fairly throughout the nation.

Holy Spirit, I am here to listen and follow you. Speak to me about each candidate and show me the candidate that God wants for this country. [Trust the Lord to speak to you and write down any revelations that the Holy Spirit reveals to you.]

_____

_____

_____

_____

_____

_____

_____

_____

_____

Wonderful Father, You said that the king's heart is like a stream of water that You direct wherever You please. For the sake of Your people in this country, please direct the heart of each candidate. Holy Spirit, please fill them with Your spirit of wisdom, understanding, counsel, courage, might, and knowledge. Equip them to produce Your will through the power of Jesus Christ, and help them to do what is pleasing to You. Convict each candidate about using ungodly campaign tactics and resorting to political mudslinging. For those candidates who do not know You as their Lord and Savior, we ask You to send people to share Your plan of salvation during campaign seasons. Father, dispatch Your angels to guard and protect their families and destroy every assignment that the devil devises against them. As we get closer to election day, create an urgency within every American voter to vote. Father, we know that nothing is too difficult for You. Miraculously, unite the Body of Christ in this country, and show us who is Your person.

Almighty God, forgive our nation for its many sins. Forgive each candidate for his sins. Forgive them for trusting in their own abilities instead of trusting in You. Forgive them for not consulting with You before making decisions or administering their authority and power. Forgive them for the times they have not been fair, compassionate, or understanding as public servants. Forgive them when they are being people pleasers and not God pleasers. We know that You look at the hearts of people instead of their outward appearances. Create in them new hearts and renew in them steadfast spirits. Forgive our government for creating a political environment that is unjust, corrupt, and immoral. Forgive us, the Body of Christ, for not praying for our leaders consistently. Forgive those American citizens who have not exercised the privilege to vote, yet complain about our country's leadership. Holy Spirit, if any of the candidates need to forgive anyone, please bring it to their remembrance and help them to forgive.

Lead our candidates not into temptation; but deliver them from the evil one.

Lord, You are the eternal King, Your rule is everlasting. All the people of the earth are nothing compared to You. All of Your acts are just and true. You alone have held the oceans in Your hand. You measured the heavens with Your fingers and know the weight of the earth. The Lord God Almighty is Your Name. In Jesus' name, amen.

Scripture References for the written text

Daniel 2:20-22, Matthew 6:10, Psalm 33:12, 1 Timothy 2:1-4, Psalm 1:1-3, Isaiah 54:17, 1 Corinthians 14:40, Proverbs 21:1, Hebrews 13:21, Psalm 91:11-12, 1 Samuel 16:7, Psalm 51:10, Daniel 4:34-35,37, Isaiah 40:12

Today, I will trust God to:

_____

_____

_____

_____

_____

_____

_____

_____

_____

Prayer Petition 15: A Prayer for the Economic Crisis in the United States of America

Scriptural Prayer

Heavenly Father, You are God, and Your Word is true. We exalt You, our God and King. We will praise Your Name forever and ever. Every day we will praise You. You are most worthy of praise. You are our source, and we place our trust in You. Holy and Righteous is Your Name. You are a great God and a great King above other gods. You are our God; we are Your people who You watch over. We are the flock under Your care. Thank You for blessing the United States of America throughout the years. Thank You, Father, for blessing the economic infrastructure of our nation. Thank You for surrounding our nation with Your favor, grace, and mercy during this time of economic crisis. Thank You for hearing the righteous as we cry out to You on behalf of our nation. Thank You, Lord, for being our source, supply, and hope.

In Jesus' name, we speak to the United States economy and all interrelated global economies and command "peace, be still" within and among all the economic systems. We stand in the authority given to us and speak to the economic infrastructure of our nation, and we command the United States credit markets to become calm and fluid. We also command all related financial intermediaries around the world to become calm and fluid. We command restoration to consumer and investor confidence. We command the banking industry to stabilize and the enterprise values of U.S. corporations to rebound supernaturally now! As a result, we decree that DOW JONES, NASDAQ, and the major financial exchange networks around the world will rebound and thrive.

We command the housing industry to stabilize and home values to be restored to levels that will reflect God's biblical promises for this country. We rebuke the spirits of conspicuous consumption, fear, uncertainty, and inefficiency. In Jesus' name, we boldly proclaim foreclosures to cease, job losses to reverse, and the stock market decline to bottom out. Peace, be still! As a church family, we confess that our Jehovah Jireh, provides all of our economic needs according to His riches by Christ Jesus. Father, we thank You in advance for Your provision. We have never seen the righteous forsaken, nor God's children begging bread. During this economic downturn, we decree that our financial position in the world is strong and healthy. We speak normalcy and balanced prosperity back into our economic system.

Eternal Father, we ask that You would pour out Your wisdom, discernment, and divine understanding into Federal Reserve Chairman Ben S. Bernanke, Treasury Secretary Henry Paulson, Barney Frank of the House Committee on Financial Services and all local, state, and national economic and government leaders. Reveal creative ideas and effective methods to them that will decrease our national deficit while continuing to provide the necessary standards, services, and benefits to the American people. Holy Spirit, stir the hearts of the Body of Christ to stand and boldly proclaim Your Word concerning the current global and U.S. economic predicament. Please restore the confidence of the American people in You, as our source and supply, and remove

any thoughts of fear or dismay. Holy Spirit, help government offi-
cials to put aside "politics" and operate in the best interest of the
American people.

Trouble the hearts of the House and Senate to approve legislation
that will provide the proper oversight and regulation that will
promote a stable and reliable economy. Almighty God, Lord of
Heaven's Armies, protect our nation during this extremely vulner-
able time in our history. Restore our international reputation and
increase Your favor for our country. We admit that we don't
deserve it, but You promise to hear our prayers and listen. Have
mercy upon our nation. We need Your divine intervention. God,
bless America!

Lord, we repent on behalf of our nation for our many sins. Forgive
us for ageism, sexism, racism, and nepotism. Forgive us for greed,
arrogance, selfishness, imperialism, and oppression. Please forgive
the financial intermediaries for charging more than they should
have charged for packaging and securitizing the mortgages. For-
give CEO's for accepting extraordinary compensation while leav-
ing Americans empty-handed. Forgive consumers who borrowed
more money than they could pay back. Forgive our nation for
financial irresponsibility and carelessness. Holy Spirit, show our
leaders who they need to forgive; and help them to forgive.

As a nation, lead us not into temptation; but deliver us from the
evil one.

Lord, there is none like You. You are great and Your Name is full
of power. Who would not fear You, O King of the nations? That
title belongs to You alone! Among all the wise people of the earth
and in all the kingdoms of the world, there is no one like You. You
are the King of glory. You are the Lord of Heaven's Armies. You
are worthy, Lord our God, to receive glory, honor, and power. You

created all things, and they exist because You created what You pleased. In Jesus's name, amen.

Scripture References for the Written Text

Psalm 145:1-2, Psalm 95:3, Psalm 100:3, Psalm 5:12, Psalm 34:17, Mark 4:39, Philippians 4:19, Psalm 37:25, James 1:5, Isaiah 41:10, Psalm 84:12, Matthew 6:13, Jeremiah 10:6-7, Psalm 24:10, Revelation 4:11

ENDNOTES

Chapter 1: Productive Prayer

1. Acts 10:34.
2. Jer. 8:22.

Chapter 2: A Definition of Prayer

1. Thess. 5:17 (NIV).
2. *Origen on Prayer*, translated by William A. Curtis, www.ccel.org/ccel/origen/prayer.i.html (accessed 5 Nov 2008).
3. John 14:6.
4. *Merriam-Webster's Collegiate Dictionary*, 10th ed., s.v. "super."
5. John 4:23-24.
6. Mal. 3:10.
7. See Exod. 7:2.
8. See Ezek. 37:1-14.
9. See John 14:10.
10. Matt. 21:12-13.
11. James 5:16.

12. James Strong, *The New Strong's Exhaustive Concordance of the Bible* (Nashville: Thomas Nelson Publishers, 1995), s.v. "energeo" (#1754).
13. *Webster's New Universal Unabridged Dictionary,* 1994, s.v. "effective."
14. *Ibid.*, s.v. "fervent."
15. Matt. 21:21-22.

Chapter 3: To Whom Do We Pray?

1. Ps. 102:12.
2. Ps. 90:2.
3. Ps. 62:11.
4. Jer. 32:17.
5. Ps. 139:7-10.
6. Ps. 147:5.
7. Ps. 145:17.
8. Deut. 32:4.
9. Heb. 13:8.
10. Acts 10:34.
11. See Gen. 22:17.

Chapter 4: The Power Source

1. 2 Tim. 3:16-17.
2. See Ps. 19:7-11.
3. James Strong, *The New Strong's Exhaustive Concordance of the Bible* (Nashville: Thomas Nelson Publishers, 1995), s.v. "theópneustos" (#2315).
4. Gen. 2:7.
5. John 1:1-5.
6. 1 John 5:7.
7. Rev. 19:13.
8. John 1:14.
9. John 1:3.

10. James Strong, s.v. "lógos" (#3056).
11. Matt. 6:7.
12. 2 Tim. 3:16-17.
13. *Merriam-Webster's Collegiate Dictionary*, 10th ed., s.v. "profitable."
14. *Webster's New Universal Unabridged Dictionary*, 1994, s.v. "teach."
15. *Ibid.*, s.v. "reprove."
16. Rom. 12:2.
17. Matt. 4:4,7,10.
18. Luke 10:19.
19. Heb. 4:12-13.
20. Ps. 147:15.
21. Prov. 18:21.
22. James Strong, s.v. "psuchc" (#5590).
23. *BibleWorks 7*, CD-ROM, version 7, BibleWorks.
24. James Strong, *Strong's Exhaustive Concordance of the Bible* (Nashville: Thomas Nelson Publishers, 1995), s.v. "pncuma" (#4151).
25. James Strong, s.v. "aletheia" (#0225).
26. *BibleWorks 7*, CD-ROM, version 7, BibleWorks.
27. *Merriam-Webster's Collegiate Dictionary*, 10th ed., s.v. "true."
28. John 17:13-18.
29. Rom. 12:1-2
30. Ps. 119:105.
31. Isa. 55:10-11.
32. Heb. 11:3.
33. Gen. 1:3.
34. Ps. 107:20.
35. Prov. 4:20-22.
36. Matt. 4:4.
37. Heb. 4:12.
38. Isa. 55:11.

Chapter 5: Pray "The Model Prayer"—Part I

1. Luke 11:1.
2. William Barclay, *The Lord's Prayer* (Louisville: Westminster John Knox Press, 1999), 5.
3. Marvin R. Wilson, *Our Father Abraham* (Grand Rapids: Wm.B. Eerdmans Publishing Co., 1989), 157.
4. *Ibid.*
5. See Matt. 6:9-13.
6. Matt. 6:7.
7. See James 5:16.
8. Heb. 4:16.
9. See Eph. 1:5.
10. See John 1:12.
11. See Gal. 4:28.
12. Lev. 22:29.
13. Ps. 26:6-7.
14. Ps. 50:14.
15. Ps. 95:2.
16. Ps. 107:22.
17. Ps. 33:1.
18. William Barclay, *The Lord's Prayer* (Louisville: Westminster John Knox Press, 1999), 39-40.
19. *Ibid.*, 39
20. *Ibid.*, 38.
21. *Ibid.*, 40-41.
22. Ps. 100:1-2.

Chapter 6: Pray "The Model Prayer"—Part II

1. See Gen. 2:15.
2. See Gen. 12:2.
3. See Exod. 6:10.
4. See Judg. 4:9.
5. See 2 Sam. 7:12-13.

6. See 1 Kings 5:5.

7. See Luke 1:30-31.

8. See John 10:9.

9. 1 John 5:14-15.

10. James Strong, *The New Strong's Exhaustive Concordance of the Bible* (Nashville: Thomas Nelson Publishers, 1995), s.v. "aiteo" (#154).

11. See Matt. 6:33.

12. See 1 Tim. 2:1-2.

13. William Barclay, *The Lord's Prayer* (Louisville: Westminster John Knox Press, 1999), 75.

14. *Ibid.*, 78

15. *Ibid.*, 78.

16. *Ibid.*, 79.

17. *Ibid.*, 80.

18. Brad Young, *The Jewish Background to the Lord's Prayer* (Dayton: Center for Judaic Christian Studies, 1984), 26.

19. Prov. 3:5-6.

20. Warren W. Wiersbe, *Classic Sermons on the Lord's Prayer* (Grand Rapids: Kregel Publications, 2000), 106 (Sermon by George H. Morrison).

Chapter 7: Pray "The Model Prayer"—Part III

1. William Barclay, *The Lord's Prayer* (Louisville: Westminster John Knox Press, 1999), 86.

2. John 10:10.

3. Prov. 16:24 (NLT).

4. William Barclay, 97.

5. *Ibid.*, 99.

6. *Ibid.*, 99.

7. See 1 Cor. 10:13.

8. James Strong, *The New Strong's Exhaustive Concordance of the Bible* (Nashville: Thomas Nelson Publishers, 1995), s.v. "peirasmos" (#3986).
9. See Gen. 22.
10. Gen. 22:7.
11. Gen. 22:8.
12. 1 Pet. 5:8.
13. Gen. 3:1 (NLT).

Chapter 8: Walk the Talk

1. Kirbyjon Caldwell, prayer at the 55th Presidential Inauguration for George W. Bush, January 20, 2005.
2. Prayer Examples 6 and 7 were adapted from prayers written for Windsor Village United Methodist Church.

Chapter 9: Pray-ers With Mountain-Moving Faith

1. James Strong, *The New Strong's Exhaustive Concordance of the Bible* (Nashville: Thomas Nelson Publishers, 1995), s.v. "pistis" (#4102).
2. 1 Cor. 1:9.
3. 1 Cor. 10:13.
4. 2 Thess. 3:3.
5. Heb. 12:2.
6. Exod. 3:9-14.
7. Exod. 5:1-2.
8. Exod. 6:10-13.
9. Exod. 8:1-2, 20-21.
10. Exod. 10:3-4.
11. Heb. 11:7.
12. Heb. 11:8-10.
13. Dan. 3:17-18.
14. Rom. 10:17.
15. Eph. 1:13.

16. Luke 1:38.
17. Heb. 11:6.
18. James 2:23.

Chapter 10: Prayer and Results

1. See Rom. 4:17.
2. See Ps. 145:3; Ps. 24:1; Ps. 93:1-2; Phil. 4:13; Ps. 1:3; Deut. 28:6; Matt. 6:13; 1 Tim. 1:1.

ABOUT THE AUTHOR

Pastor Suzette Caldwell serves as the Board Chair and President of the Kingdom Builders' Prayer Institute (The Prayer Institute), a community-based outreach organization whose mission is to pray strategic, Bible-based prayers that will establish God's Kingdom on earth as He has purposed it in Heaven. The Prayer Institute serves as a spiritual outlet to communicate the plans and strategies of God and destroy the plans and strategies of satan.

In the 21st century, it is imperative for the Church to develop a consistent, progressive, strategic system of prayer. The Prayer Institute is committed to doing its part by developing and executing prayer systems that will transform the supernatural plans of God into our earthly realities.

We believe that all believers have the capacity to pray in a way that will change their world. We provide training seminars and conferences to empower leaders and lay persons to accomplish God's will for their lives. Additionally, The Prayer Institute is available to provide consultation to churches and Christian organizations who want to start powerful prayer ministries or enhance their existing prayer ministries.

To schedule seminars, conferences, speaking engagements, or prayer consulting contact:

Kingdom Builders' Prayer Institute
Attn: Pastor Suzette Caldwell
6011 W. Orem
Houston, TX 77085
prayerinstitute.com

or

Windsor Village United Methodist Church
Attn: Pastor Suzette Caldwell
6011 W. Orem
Houston, TX 77085
Kingdombuilders.com

Additional copies of this book and other
book titles from DESTINY IMAGE are
available at your local bookstore.

Call toll-free: 1-800-722-6774.

Send a request for a catalog to:

Destiny Image® Publishers, Inc.
P.O. Box 310
Shippensburg, PA 17257-0310

*"Speaking to the Purposes of God for This
Generation and for the Generations to Come."*

**For a complete list of our titles,
visit us at www.destinyimage.com.**